Praise for *When Atheism Beco...*
(Formerly titled *I Do...*)

"Provocative."

"Hedges brings a powerfully equ... ...rong credibility to his call to have this new movement carefully scrutinized."

—*The Globe and Mail*

"If he is right—and there is much in this book that is compelling—we will soon be faced with a dire new world order, or disorder."

—*The Atlanta Journal-Constitution*

"A well-timed response to the recent shelf of new books extolling atheism."

—*Sun-Sentinel*

Praise for *American Fascists*

"Chris Hedges may be the most credible figure yet to detect real-life fascism in the Red America of megachurches, gay-marriage bans and Left Behind books. *American Facists* is at its most daring when it enunciates . . . the perversities that are obvious to those of us not beholden to political exigencies."

—*New York Observer*

"*American Fascists* . . . is a call to arms against what Hedges sees as the efforts of Jerry Falwell, Pat Robertson, and the operators of Trinity Broadcasting Network, among others, to turn the United States into a Christian nation. Hedges reports in fascinating detail what goes on inside churches, conventions, and meeting halls of the Christian right."

—*Los Angeles Times*

"This is a powerful book that looks inside some of the darkest movements on American soil."

—*Time Out New York*

Praise for *Losing Moses on the Freeway*

"Telling his own story, Mr. Hedges writes better than anyone else in the game, without sentiment but full of love and hate . . . He walks out of these pages as a good enough man—better than most, perhaps—but best of all, he emerges as a teller of human tales with the unusual capacity to get them right."

—*New York Observer*

"At a time when the mere mention of religion can excite so much passion, anxiety, and discord, Chris Hedges' *Losing Moses on the Freeway* offers a sane and bracing way to think about, and rethink, the whole subject of faith. Each of the deeply felt essays finds spirit lessons in the most unlikely places."

—*O, The Oprah Magazine*

"Hedges brings a broad and secular perspective to a deep examination of the principles of the Ten Commandments. He turns a sharp eye toward a variety of human experiences touching on elements of the commandments in ways that are uncommon and insightful . . . A deeply insightful and moving book."

—*Booklist*

Praise for *War Is a Force That Gives Us Meaning*

"A brilliant, thoughtful, timely and unsettling book . . . it will rattle jingoists, pacifists, moralists, nihilists, politicians and professional soldiers equally . . . Abounds with Hedges' harrowing and terribly moving eyewitness accounts . . . Powerful and informative."

—*The New York Times Book Review*

"[A] powerful chronicle of modern war . . . A persuasive call for humility and realism in the pursuit of national goals by force of arms . . . A potent and eloquent warning."
—*The New York Times*

"The best kind of war journalism: It is bitterly poetic and ruthlessly philosophical. It sends out a powerful message to people contemplating the escalation of the 'war against terrorism.'"
—*Los Angeles Times*

"A compelling read and a valuable counterweight to the more antiseptic discussions common among strategic analysts."
—*Foreign Affairs*

"This should be required reading in this post-9/11 world as we debate the possibility of war with Iraq."
—*Publishers Weekly*

"Chris Hedges has written a powerful book, one which bears sad witness to what veterans have long understood . . . [A] somber and timely warning to those—in any society—who would evoke the emotions of war for the pursuit of political gain."
—General Wesley K. Clark, former Supreme Allied Commander, Europe, and author of *Waging Modern War*

"No one is in a better position than Hedges to pronounce on the revolting things war does to everyone caught up in it . . . A confession of rare and frightening honesty."
—Slate.com

ALSO BY CHRIS HEDGES

American Fascists

Losing Moses on the Freeway

What Every Person Should Know About War

War Is a Force That Gives Us Meaning

WHEN ATHEISM BECOMES RELIGION

AMERICA'S NEW FUNDAMENTALISTS

CHRIS HEDGES

Previously published as
I Don't Believe in Atheists

FREE PRESS
New York London Toronto Sydney

A Division of Simon & Schuster, Inc.
1230 Avenue of the Americas
New York, NY 10020

First Free Press trade paperback edition March 2009

FREE PRESS and colophon are trademarks
of Simon & Schuster, Inc.

For information about special discounts for bulk purchases,
please contact Simon & Schuster Special Sales at 1-800-456-6798
or business@simonandschuster.com

Manufactured in the United States of America

1   3   5   7   9   10   8   6   4   2

The Library of Congress has cataloged the hardcover edition
as follows:

Hedges, Chris.
I don't believe in atheists / by Chris Hedges.
p. cm.
1. Religion.   2. Atheism.   3. Good and evil.
4. Religion and science.   I. Title.
BL85.H35   2008
211—dc22   2007039173

ISBN-13: 978-1-4165-6795-0
ISBN-10:   1-4165-6795-X
ISBN-13: 978-1-4165-7078-3 (pbk)
ISBN-10:   1-4165-7078-0 (pbk)

All Biblical quotations taken from the English Standard Bible.

Originally published in hardcover as *I Don't Believe in Atheists*
by Free Press

For my wife, Eunice Wong,
whose love is the eternal rocks beneath,
the clear natural light,
life itself

CONTENTS

What yesterday was still religion, is no longer such today; and what today is atheism, tomorrow will be religion.

—Ludwig Feuerbach[1]

PROLOGUE

I flew to Los Angeles from Philadelphia in May of 2007 to debate Sam Harris, the author of *The End of Faith* and *Letter to a Christian Nation*, in UCLA's cavernous Royce Hall. I debated Christopher Hitchens, who wrote *God Is Not Great*, two days later in San Francisco. This book is a product of those confrontations.

I paid little attention, until these two public debates, to the positions of such thinkers, who sometimes are called, or call themselves, "new atheists." After all, there is nothing intrinsically moral about being a believer or a nonbeliever. There are many people of great moral probity and courage who seek meaning outside of formal religious structures, who reject religious language and religious ritual and define themselves as atheists. There are also many religious figures that in the name of one god or another sanctify intolerance, repression and violence.

The agenda of the new atheists, however, is disturbing. These atheists embrace a belief system as intolerant, chauvinistic and bigoted as that of religious fundamentalists. They propose a route to collective salvation and the moral advancement of the human species through science and reason. The utopian dream of a perfect society and a perfect human being, the idea that we are moving toward collective salvation, is one of the most dangerous legacies of the Christian faith and the Enlightenment. All too often throughout history, those who believed in the possibility of this perfection (variously defined) have called for the silencing or eradication of human beings who are impediments to human progress. They turn their particular notion of the good into an inflexible standard of universal good. They prove blind to their own corruption and capacity for evil. They soon commit evil not for evil's sake but to make a better world.

I started Harris's book when it was published but put it aside. His facile attack on a form of religious belief we all hate, his childish simplicity and ignorance of world affairs, as well as his demonization of Muslims, made the book tedious, at its best, and often idiotic and racist. His assertion, for example, that the war in the former Yugoslavia was caused by religion was ridiculous. As the Balkan Bureau Chief for *The New York Times*, I was in the former Yugoslavia, including in the Bosnian capital Sarajevo when it was under siege. While religious institutions and their leaders enthusiastically signed on for the slaughter directed by ethnic nationalist leaders in Zagreb, Belgrade and Sarajevo, religion had nothing to do with the war. The war had far more to do with the economic collapse of Yugoslavia than with religion or ancient ethnic hatreds. His assertion that Muslim parents welcome the death of children as suicide bombers could only have been written by someone who never sat in the home of a grieving mother and father in Gaza who have just lost their child. I did not take Harris seriously. This was a mistake.

Harris, as well as atheists from Hitchens to Richard Dawkins to Daniel Dennett, has found a following among people disgusted with the chauvinism, intolerance, anti-intellectualism and self-righteousness of religious fundamentalists. I share this disgust. I wrote a book called *American Fascists: The Christian Right and the War on America.* The Christian Right in the United States is the most frightening mass movement in American history. We dislike the same people. But we do not dislike them for the same reasons. This is not a small difference.

I was raised in a church where my father, a Presbyterian minister, spent his career speaking out, often at some personal cost, in support of the civil rights movement, the Vietnam antiwar movement and the gay rights movement. The religious figures I studied and the ones I sought to emulate when I was a seminarian at Harvard Divinity School, included Martin Luther King Jr., Dorothy Day, William Sloane Coffin Jr., Archbishop Oscar Romero of El Salvador, and Daniel Berrigan. It was possible to admire these men and women and what they stood for, yet hold institutional religion in little regard. It was possible to find in the Christian faith meaning and purpose while acknowledging the flaws in the Christian system and rejecting the morally indefensible passages in the Bible. Religion, as Reinhold Niebuhr pointed out, is a good thing for good people and a bad thing for bad people.

The institutional church has often used its power and religious authority to sanctify cruelty and exclusion. The self-righteous smugness and suffocating piety of religious leaders, along with the habit of speaking on behalf of people they never meet, are characteristic of many liberal and conservative churches. The church often likes the poor but doesn't like the smell of the poor. I graduated from seminary and decided, largely because of my distaste for the hypocrisy of the church, not to get ordained. I left the United States to report on the conflicts in Central America. I rarely go to church now and when I do often roll my eyes at the inanity of the sermons and the arrogance of many of the congregants, who appear to believe they are "honorary" sinners. The liberal church, attacked by atheists as an ineffectual "moderate" religion and by fundamentalists as a "nominal" form of Christianity, is, as its critics point out, a largely vapid and irrelevant force. It may not support the violent projects of apocalyptic killing championed by atheists such as Harris or Hitchens—or by some Christian radicals—but it also does not understand how the world works or the seduction of evil. The liberal church is a largely middle-class, bourgeois phenomenon, filled with many people who have profited from industrialization, the American empire, and global capitalism. They often seem to think that if "we" can be nice and inclusive, everything will work out. The liberal church also usually buys into the myth that we can morally progress as a species. It, too, accepts, along with the atheists and the fundamentalists, Pangloss's rosy vision in Voltaire's *Candide* that we live in "the best of all possible worlds" ("*ce meilleur des mondes possibles*") and that if we have faith and trust in the forces around us, "all is for the best" ("*tout est au mieux*"). It is this naïve belief in our goodness and decency—this inability to face the dark reality of human nature, our capacity for evil and the morally neutral universe we inhabit—that is the most disturbing aspect of all of these belief systems. There is nothing in human nature or human history to support the idea that we are morally advancing as a species or that we will overcome the flaws of human nature. We progress technologically and scientifically, but not morally. We use the newest instruments of technological and scientific progress to create more efficient forms of killing, repression, economic exploitation and to accelerate environmental degradation. There is a good and a bad side to human progress. We are not advancing toward a glorious utopia.

Religious institutions, however, should be separated from the religious values imparted to me by religious figures, including my father. Most of these men and women ran afoul of their own religious authorities. Religion, real religion, involved fighting for justice, standing up for the voiceless and the weak, reaching out in acts of kindness and compassion to the stranger and the outcast, living a life of simplicity, cultivating empathy and defying the powerful. It was a commitment to care for the other. Spirituality was defined not by "how it is with me," but rather by the tougher spirituality of resistance, the spirituality born of struggle, of the fight with the world's evils. This spirituality, vastly different from the narcissism of modern spirituality movements, was eloquently articulated by King and the Lutheran minister Dietrich Bonhoeffer, who was imprisoned and put to death by the Nazis.

Too many of the new atheists, like the Christian fundamentalists, support the imperialist projects and preemptive wars of the United States as necessities in the battle against terrorism and irrational religion. They divide the world into superior and inferior races, those who are enlightened by reason and knowledge, and those who are governed by irrational and dangerous religious beliefs. Hitchens and Harris describe the Muslim world, where I spent seven years, most of them as the Middle East Bureau Chief for *The New York Times*, in language that is as racist, crude and intolerant as that used by Pat Robertson or Jerry Falwell. They are a secular version of the religious right. They misuse the teachings of Charles Darwin and evolutionary biology just as the Christian fundamentalists misuse the Bible. They are anti-intellectual. And while the new atheists do not have the power of the Christian Right and are not a threat to the democratic state as the Christian Right is, they do engage in the same chauvinism and call for the same violent utopianism. They sell this under secular banners. They believe, like the Christian Right, that we are moving forward to a paradise, a state of human perfection, this time made possible by science and reason. They argue, like the Christian radicals, that some human beings, maybe many human beings, have to be eradicated to achieve this better world. They see only one truth: their truth. Human beings must become like them, think like them and adopt their values, which they insist are universal, or be banished from civilized society. All other values, which they never investigate or examine, are dismissed.

These atheists and Christian radicals have built squalid little belief systems that are in the service of themselves and their own power. They urge us forward into a non–reality-based world, one where force and violence, self-exaltation and blind nationalism are unquestioned goods. They seek to make us afraid of what we do not know or understand. They use this fear to justify cruelty and war. They ask us to kneel before little idols that look and act like them, telling us that one day, if we trust enough in God or reason, we will have everything we desire.

This book is a call to reject simplistic utopian visions. It is a call to accept the ineluctable limitations of being human. It is a call to face reality, a reality which in the coming decades is going to be bleak and difficult. Those who are blinded by utopian visions inevitably turn to force to make their impos-

sible dreams and their noble ideals real. They believe the
ends, no matter how barbaric, justify the means. Utopian
ideologues, armed with the technology and mechanisms of
industrial slaughter, have killed tens of millions of people
over the last century. They ask us to inflict suffering and
death in the name of virtue and truth. The recent crop of
atheists, in the end, offer us a new version of an old and dangerous faith. It is one we have seen before. It is one we
must fight.

Chris Hedges
Princeton, New Jersey

CHAPTER ONE

The God Debate

"The shudder of awe is humanity's highest faculty,
Even though this world is forever altering values . . ."
—Goethe, Faust [1]

We live in an age of faith. We are assured we are advancing as a species toward a world that will be made perfect by reason, technology, science or the second coming of Jesus Christ. Evil can be eradicated. War has been declared on nebulous forces or cultures that stand as impediments to progress. Religion (if you are secular) is blamed for genocide, injustice, persecution, backwardness and intellectual and sexual repression. "Secular humanism" (if you are born again) is branded as a tool of Satan. The folly of humankind, however, is pervasive. It infects all human endeavors. Institutional religion or the cults of science and reason are not exempt.

The greatest danger that besets us does not come from believers or atheists; it comes from those who, under the guise of religion, science or reason, imagine that we can free ourselves from the limitations of human nature and perfect the human species. Those who insist we are morally advancing as a species are deluding themselves. There is little in science or history to support this idea. Human individuals can make moral advances, as can human societies, but they also make moral reverses. Our personal and collective histories are not linear. We alternate between periods of light and periods of darkness. We can move forward materially, but we do not move forward morally. The belief in collective moral advancement ignores the inherent flaws in human nature as well as the tragic reality of human history. Whether it comes in secular or religious form, this belief is magical thinking. The secular version of this myth peddles fables no less fantastic, and no less delusional, than those preached from church pulpits. The battle under way in America is not a battle between religion and science; it is a battle between religious and secular fundamentalists. It is a battle between two groups intoxicated with the utopian and magical belief that humankind can master its destiny. This is one of the most pervasive forms of self-delusion, as Marcel Proust understood, but it has disastrous consequences. It encourages us to ignore reality.

"The soldier is convinced that a certain interval of time, capable of being indefinitely prolonged, will be allowed him before the bullet finds him, the thief before he is caught, men in general before they have to die," Proust wrote. "That is the amulet which preserves people—and sometimes peoples—not from danger but from the fear of danger, in reality from the belief in danger, which in certain cases allows them to brave it without actually needing to be brave."[2]

The word *utopia* was coined by Thomas More in 1516 from the Greek words for *no* and *place*. To be a utopian, to live for the creation of a fantastic and unreal world, was to live in no place, to remove oneself from reality. It is only by building an ethic based on reality, one that takes into account the dangers and limits of the human situation, that we can begin to adjust our behavior to cope with social, environmental and political problems. All utopian schemes of impossible advances and glorious conclusions end in squalor and fanaticism. The current "war on terror" by the United States is one such scheme. It is being fought so that evil can be violently uprooted. Its proponents promise a world that will become "reasonable," a "civil" world ruled by the "rational" forces of global capitalism. Those who support the war on terror speak as if victory in any tangible sense is possible. This noble vision of a harmonious world is used to justify violence and war, to turn us into criminals who carry out needless murder and torture in the name of human progress.

The desire for emancipation, universal happiness and prosperity has a seductive pull on the human imagination. It preoccupied the early church, which was infused with exclusivist utopian sects. We are comforted by the thought that we progress morally as a species. We want things to get better. We want to believe we are moving forward. This hope is more reassuring than reality. All the signs in our present world point to a coming anarchy, a massive dislocation of populations resulting from ecological devastation and climate change, multiple pollutions, the weight of over-population and wars fought over dwindling natural resources. Science, which should be used to address these looming disasters, has largely become a tool of corporations that seek not to protect us but to make a profit and stimulate the economy. New, potentially threatening technologies, such as genetically modified organisms and nanotechnologies, are being unleashed with no understanding of the impact on the biosphere. The global population is expected to jump from 2 billion in 1927 to 9 billion people by 2045,[3] which means that if this growth is left unchecked, we will no longer be able to sustain ourselves, especially as nations such as China seek the consumption levels of the industrialized nations in Europe and North America. Nearly two thirds of the life-support services provided to us by nature are already in precipitous decline worldwide. The old wars of conquest, expansion and exploitation will be replaced by wars fought for the necessities of air, food, sustainable living conditions and water. And as we race toward this catastrophe, scientists continue to make discoveries, set these discoveries upon us and walk away from the impact.

Yet the belief persists that science and reason will save us;

it persists because it makes it possible to ignore or minimize these catastrophes. We drift toward disaster with the comforting thought that the god of science will intervene on our behalf. We prefer to think we are the culmination of a process, the result of centuries of human advancement, rather than creatures unable to escape from the irrevocable follies and blunders of human nature. The idea of inevitable progress allows us to place ourselves at the center of creation, to exalt ourselves. It translates our narrow self-interest into a universal good. But it is irresponsible. It permits us to avert our eyes from reality and trust in an absurdist faith.

"For every age," Joseph Conrad wrote, "is fed on illusions, lest men should renounce life early and the human race come to an end."[4]

The belief that rational and quantifiable disciplines such as science can be used to perfect human society is no less absurd than a belief in magic, angels and divine intervention. Scientific methods, part of the process of changing the material world, are nearly useless in the nebulous world of politics, ideas, values and ethics. But the belief in collective moral progress is a seductive one. It is what has doomed populations in the past who have chased after impossible dreams, and it threatens to doom us again. It is, at its core, the enticing delusion that we can be more than human, that we can become gods.

We have nothing to fear from those who do or do not believe in God; we have much to fear from those who do not believe in sin. The concept of sin is a stark acknowledgment that we can never be omnipotent, that we are bound and limited by human flaws and self-interest. The concept of sin is a check on the utopian dreams of a perfect world. It prevents us from believing in our own perfectibility or the illusion that the material advances of science and technology equal an intrinsic moral improvement in our species. To turn away from God is harmless. Saints have been trying to do it for centuries. To turn away from sin is catastrophic. Religious fundamentalists, who believe they know and can carry out the will of God, disregard their severe human limitations. They act as if they are free from sin. The secular utopians of the twenty-first century have also forgotten they are human. These two groups peddle absolutes. Those who do not see as they see, speak as they speak and act as they act are worthy only of conversion or eradication.

We discard the wisdom of sin at our peril. Sin reminds us that all human beings are flawed—though not equally flawed. Sin is the acceptance that there will never be a final victory over evil, that the struggle for morality is a battle that will always have to be fought. Studies in cognitive behavior illustrate the accuracy and wisdom of this Biblical concept. Human beings are frequently irrational. They are governed by unconscious forces, many of them self-destructive. This understanding of innate human corruptibility and human limitations, whether explained by the theologian Augustine or the psychoanalyst Sigmund Freud, has been humankind's most potent check on utopian visions. It has forced human beings to accept their own myopia and irrationality, to acknowledge that no act, even one defined as moral or virtuous, is free from the taint of self-interest and corruption. We are bound by our animal natures.

The question is not whether God exists. It is whether we contemplate or are utterly indifferent to the transcendent, that which cannot be measured or quantified, that which lies beyond the reach of rational deduction. We all encounter this aspect of existence, in love, beauty, alienation, loneliness, suffering, good, evil and the reality of death. These powerful, non rational, super-real forces in human life are the domain of religion. All cultures have struggled to give words to these mysteries and moments of transcendence. God—and different cultures have given God many names and many attributes—is that which works upon us and through us to find meaning and relevance in a morally neutral universe. Religion is our finite, flawed and imperfect expression of the infinite. The experience of transcendence—the struggle to acknowledge the infinite—need not be attributed to an external being called God. As Karen Armstrong and others have pointed out, the belief in a personal God can, in fact, be antireligious. But the religious impulse addresses something just as concrete as the pursuit of scientific or historical knowledge: it addresses the human need for the sacred. God is, as Thomas Aquinas argues, the power that allows us to be ourselves. God is a search, a way to frame the questions. God is a call to reverence.

Human beings come ingrained with this impulse. Buddhists speak of nirvana in words that are nearly identical to those employed by many monotheists to describe God. This impulse asks: What are we? Why are we here? What, if anything, are we supposed to do? What does it all mean?

Science and reason, while they can illuminate these questions, can definitively answer none of them.

This impulse, this need for the sacred, propels human beings to create myths and stories that explain who they are, where they came from, and their place in the cosmos. Myth is not a primitive scientific theory that can be discarded in an industrialized age. We all stoke and feed the fires of symbolic mythic narratives, about our nation, our times and ourselves, to give meaning, coherence and purpose to our lives. The danger arises when the myths we tell about ourselves endow us with divine power, when we believe that it is our role to shape and direct human destiny, for then we seek to become gods. We can do this in the name of Jesus Christ, Muhammad or Western civilization. The result, for those who defy us, is the same—repression and often death. The refusal to acknowledge human limitations and our irrevocable flaws can thus cross religious and secular lines to feed both religious fundamentalism and the idolization of technology, reason and science.

The language of science and reason is now used by many atheists to express the ancient longings for human perfectibility. According to them, reason and science, rather than religion, will regulate human conflicts and bring about a paradise. This vision draws its inspiration from the Enlightenment, the European intellectual movement of the seventeenth and eighteenth centuries that taught that reason and scientific method could be applied to all aspects of human life. This application would lead to progress, human enlightenment and a better world. René Descartes, David Hume, John Locke, Voltaire, Immanuel Kant, Denis Diderot, Jean-Jacques Rousseau and Thomas Paine bequeathed to us this godless religion.

The Enlightenment was a curse and a blessing. Its proponents championed human dignity and condemned tyranny, superstition, ignorance and injustice. Because French philosophers including Voltaire, Rousseau and Diderot, who influenced the ideologues of the French Revolution, called for social and political justice, the Enlightenment led to the emancipation of Jews in Western Europe, freeing them from squalid ghettos. But there was a dark side to the Enlightenment. Philosophers insisted that the universe and human nature could be understood and controlled by the rational mind. They saw the universe as ruled exclusively by consistent laws such as Isaac Newton's law of gravity or Galileo's law of falling bodies. These laws could be explained mathematically or scientifically. The human species, elevated above animals because it possessed the capacity to reason, could break free of its animal nature and, through reason, understand itself and the world. It could make wise and informed decisions for the betterment of humanity. The disparity between the rational person and the instinctive, irrational person, these philosophers argued, would be solved through education and knowledge.

The Enlightenment empowered those who argued that superstition, blind instinct and ignorance had to be eradicated. Kant, in *Anthropology from a Pragmatic Point of View*, published in 1798, asserted that Africans were inherently predisposed to slavery. Thus the Enlightenment gave the world the "scientific racism" adopted as an ideological veneer for murder by nineteenth- and twentieth-century despots. Those who could not be educated and reformed, radical Enlightenment thinkers began to argue, should be eliminated so they could no longer poison human society. The Jacobins who seized control during the French Revolution were the first in a long line of totalitarian monsters who justified murder by invoking supposedly enlightened ideals. Their radical experiment in human engineering was embodied in the Republic of Virtue and the Reign of Terror, which saw 17,000 people executed. Belief in the moral superiority of Western civilization allowed the British to wipe out the Tasmanian Aborigines. British hunting parties were given licenses to exterminate this "inferior race," whom the colonial authorities said should be "hunted down like wild beasts and destroyed." The British captured many in traps and burned or tortured them to death. The same outlook led to the slaughter of the Caribs of the Caribbean, the Guanches of the Canary Islands, as well as Native Americans. It justified the slave trade that abducted 15 million Africans and killed even more. And it was this long tradition of colonial genocide in the name of progress in places like King Leopold's Congo that set the stage for the industrial-scale killing of the Holocaust and man-made famines of the Soviet Union.

Reigns of terror are thus the bastard children of the Enlightenment. Terror in the name of utopian ideals would rise again and again in the coming centuries. The Nazi death camps and the Soviet gulags were spawned by the Enlightenment. Fascists and communists were bred on visions of human perfectibility. Tens of millions of people have been murdered in the futile effort to reform human nature and build utopian societies. During these reigns of terror, science and reason served, as they continue to serve, interests purportedly devoted to the common good—and to vast mechanisms of repression and mass killing.

The belief in human perfectibility, in history as a march toward a glorious culmination, is malformed theology. It permits wild, eschatological visions to be built under religious or secular banners. This dangerous belief colors the thought of the new crop of atheist writers. They will tell us what is right and wrong, not in the eyes of God, but according to the purity of the rational mind. They, too, seek to destroy those who do not conform to their vision. They, too, wrap their intolerance in Enlightenment virtues.

"Some propositions are so dangerous that it may even be ethical to kill people for believing them," Sam Harris writes. "This may seem an extraordinary claim, but it merely enunciates an ordinary fact about the world in which we live. Certain beliefs place their adherents beyond the reach of every peaceful means of persuasion, while inspiring them to commit acts of extraordinary violence against others. There is, in fact, no talking to some people. If they cannot be captured, and they often cannot, otherwise tolerant people may be justified in killing them in self-defense. This is what the United States attempted in Afghanistan, and it is what we and other Western powers are bound to attempt, at an even greater cost to ourselves and to innocents abroad, elsewhere in the Muslim world. We will continue to spill blood in what is, at bottom, a war of ideas."[5]

Any form of knowledge that claims to be absolute ceases to be knowledge. It becomes a form of faith. Harris mistakes a tiny subset of criminals and terrorists for one billion Muslims. He justifies the unjustifiable in the name of civilization. The passions of atheists like Harris, hidden under the jargon of reason and science, are as bankrupt as the passions of Christian and Islamic fundamentalists who sanctify mass slaughter in the name of their utopias. Religious fundamentalists pervert and distort religion to serve their own fears and aggrandize themselves. Atheists such as Harris do the same with science and reason.

The dangerous myth that confuses moral progress with material progress permits us to believe we have discovered a way out of the human predicament. It places faith in an empowered elite to guide us toward a new world. Science increases not only our power to protect life and encourage virtue, but also our capacity to inflict death and destruction. The industrial slaughter and genocides of the past century were all products of the Enlightenment and their satellite ideologies, from liberal imperialism to communism to fascism. All preached collective moral progress through exploitation, repression and violence. All were utopian. And all unleashed science and technology, in the service of war and profit, to kill human beings on a scale unseen in human history. The Enlightenment vision, because it renders all other values subservient to reason and science, allows us to divide the human species into superior and inferior breeds. It sanctifies inhumane abuse of the weak to push the human race forward. This corruption was built into the Enlightenment from its inception. The Enlightenment may have encouraged an admirable humanism, but it also led to undreamt-of genocide and totalitarian repression.

Those who offer collective salvation, whether through science, Jesus Christ or Muhammad, promise an unattainable human paradise. They embrace the Christian conception of time as linear, the idea that we are moving toward revelation and paradise. The difference—and it is a vast one—is that human beings, rather than God, will make this final victory possible. This Enlightenment religion has dominated the last century. These utopian visions, often after a great deal of death and suffering, always fail. They will fail once again.

Those who believe in collective moral progress define this progress by their own narrow historical, cultural, linguistic and social experience. They see "the other" as equal only when the other is identical to themselves. They project their own values on the rest of the human race. These secular and religious fundamentalists are egocentrics unable to accept human difference. Those who are different do not need to be investigated, understood or tolerated, for they are intellectually and morally inferior. Those who are different are imperfect versions of themselves.

These secular utopians, like Christian fundamentalists, are stunted products of a self-satisfied, materialistic middle class. They seek in their philosophical systems a moral justification for their own comfort, self-absorption and power. They do not question the imperial projects of the nation, globalization or the vast disparities in wealth and security between themselves, as members of the world's industrialized elite, and the rest of the human race. Philosophy, like theology, is often in the service of power. This creed is no exception.

"And I say to the Christians while I'm at it, 'Go love your own enemies; by the way, don't be loving mine,' " Christopher Hitchens, the author of *God Is Not Great,* said when I debated him in San Francisco. "I think the enemies of civilization should be beaten and killed and defeated, and I don't make any apology for it. And I think it's sickly and stupid and suicidal to say that we should love those who hate us and try to kill us and our children and burn our libraries and destroy our society. I have no patience with this nonsense."

The rise of religious fundamentalism has been a spur to many decent, skeptical people who find religious bigotry, superstition and intolerance repugnant. This has made them receptive to antireligious polemics. Atheism, unlike Christian fundamentalism, has not wormed its way into the corridors of power or built an alliance with the corporate state to dismantle American democracy. Atheists, unlike the Christian radicals, have not set up frightening systems of indoctrination through television, radio, schools and colleges. Atheists have not mounted an assault against dispassionate intellectual inquiry.

But atheists such as Harris and Hitchens do offer, in place of religious fundamentalism, a surrogate religion. The battle against Christian fundamentalism, however, one of the most important struggles in the United States, is not going to be won by promoting a rival religion that also ignores human nature, is chauvinistic and intolerant, and speaks in jingoistic cant. Only an ethic that faces the reality of the coming decades, one that has already seen us disrupt the geological and biological patterns of the planet, will save us. Environmental catastrophe, and wars fought for water and oil and other natural resources will become our collective reality. Terrorism will not be eradicated. We must accept our limitations as a species and curb our wanton disregard for the interconnectedness of life. We need to investigate and understand the desperation of those who oppose us. If we continue to dismiss those who defy us as satanic, or as religious fanatics who must be silenced or eradicated, we stumble into the fundamentalist trap of a binary world of blacks and whites, a world without nuance. To explain is not to excuse. To understand is not to forgive. Those who look at others as simple, one-dimensional caricatures fuel the rage of the dispossessed. They answer violence with violence. These utopian belief systems, these forms of faith, are well-trod paths of self-delusion and self-destruction. They allow us to sleepwalk into disaster.

An atheist who accepts an irredeemable and flawed human nature, as well as a morally neutral universe, who does not think the world can be perfected by human beings, who is not steeped in cultural arrogance and feelings of superiority, who rejects the violent imperial projects under way in the Middle East, is intellectually honest. These atheists may not like the word *sin*, but they have accepted its reality. They hold an honored place in a pluralistic and diverse human community.

Atheists, including those who brought us the Enlightenment, have often been a beneficial force in the history of human thought and religion. They have forced societies to examine empty religious platitudes and hollow religious concepts. They have courageously challenged the moral hypocrisy of religious institutions. The humanistic values of the Enlightenment were a response to the abuses by organized religion, including the attempt by religious authorities to stifle intellectual and scientific freedom. Religious authorities, bought off by the elite, championed a dogmatism that sanctified the privileges and power of the ruling class. But there were always religious figures who defied their own. Many, such as the philosopher Baruch Spinoza, were branded as heretics and atheists.

The pain of living has also turned honest and compassionate men and women against God. These atheists do not believe in collective moral progress or science and reason as our ticket to salvation. They are not trying to perfect the human race. Rather, they cannot reconcile human suffering with the concept of God. This is an honest struggle. This disbelief is a form of despair, not self-exaltation.

"We then all just settled into bleak New England mourning," wrote the poet Liam Rector following the funeral of his close friend and fellow poet Jane Kenyon. "For my part, I spent a raging few years questioning how any god could let this happen, which drove me from a skeptical and buoyant agnosticism into a virulent atheism."[6]

No one has a right to question or discredit Rector's atheism. He earned it. It is an atheism that does not try and substitute itself for religion. And it does not attempt to subjugate others who have opposing beliefs.

The concept of God, even within the same religious tradition, mutates as human societies change. The reaction of nonbelievers changes with it. As Karen Armstrong writes in *A History of God*, "the idea of God formed in one generation by one set of human beings could be meaningless in another."[7] There is no immutable concept contained in the word *God*, "instead the word contains a whole spectrum of meanings, some of which are contradictory or even mutually exclusive."[8] This flexibility is what keeps the concept of God—of the divine—alive. As one conception of the divine no longer has meaning or relevance in the shifting sands of a culture, it is discarded, replaced by a new interpretation. Because there is no clear, objective definition of God, the new atheists must choose what God it is they attack. Is it the God of the mystics, the followers of the Social Gospel, the eighteenth-century deists, the Quakers, the liberation theologians, or the stern God of the patriarchs? Are they at war with Thomas Aquinas or John Calvin or Mohandas Gandhi or Thomas Merton or Paul Tillich?

These are not questions these atheists answer. They attack a religious belief of their own creation. They blame religion for the worst of human depravity, superstition and ignorance, and call on us to discard it. And once we free ourselves from religion we will be able to march forward as a species to their sunlit utopia. This is the simplistic utopian vision of human advancement shared by all fundamentalists, all those who are incapable of dealing intellectually, and perhaps emotionally, with human contradictions, limitations and ambiguities. Utopian visions of paradise, including the literal belief in heaven, are always curiously vague. This may be because a world without vice and conflict has little appeal to human beings. The atheist and religious fundamentalists perpetuate their belief systems with fear, fear of the other who seeks to destroy us and our way of life. They go into excruciating detail when speaking about the danger posed by their enemies, but slip into a dreamy vagueness when they attempt to describe their new heaven and new Earth. If we lived in a world ruled by human reason, what would it look like? Would it be a deathless life? Would we be eternally young? Would we live in monochromatic and stifling harmony? Would we all be alike in our desires and our needs? Would human suffering come to an end?

Religious understanding takes time and work. It is, as Armstrong pointed out in an interview on Salon, an art forum: "It's a way of finding meaning, like art, like painting, like poetry, in a world that is violent and cruel and often seems meaningless." Religious thought and scholarship, often belittled within many universities, is difficult and laborious: "You don't just dash off a painting. It takes years of study. I think we expect religious knowledge to be instant.

But religious knowledge comes incrementally and slowly. And religion is like any other activity. It's not easy to do it well."[9]

Those who teach that religion is evil and that science and reason will save us are as deluded as those who believe in angels and demons. They think education and knowledge will save us—but because they do not accept human limitations, they would use education as a system of indoctrination. They seek, through education, to make us conform.

Evil, however, cannot be eradicated through education. Evil will always be with us. Science and human reason, like institutional religion, have delivered as much suffering as comfort. The victims of the death camps, those killed at Hiroshima, the tens of millions who died in the Soviet gulags, or those millions of innocents maimed and killed in Vietnam, Angola, Sierra Leone, Afghanistan or Iraq and a host of other wars, know the awful truth: "The fault, dear Brutus, is not in our stars,/But in ourselves . . ."[10] There are scientists in the United States—a huge proportion of whom work for defense-related industries—constructing sophisticated weapons systems that have the capacity to exterminate millions of people. Is this a rational enterprise? Is it beneficial to humankind? Is it a reason for us to place our faith for the future of the human race in reason and science?

The story of the fall in the Garden of Eden is a warning

about the danger posed by blind faith in the power of human knowledge. The figure who delivers knowledge to Adam and Eve is the source of evil—the devil. Knowledge brings with it benefits, including self-awareness and power, but it also tempts us to play God. To act on this temptation, to worship our own capacities, lures us into utopian projects. The Biblical story of the fall conveys fundamental truths about freedom, guilt, our relation to nature and mortality. Those who formulated religious myths imparted an important spiritual truth rather than a historical or scientific fact. Those who created the Greek myths, the Vedas, the Upanishads, as well as the Bible, were trying to explain human beings to human beings.

We carry on a never-ending struggle with "the evil that I would not that I do," as Paul wrote. It is this capacity for empathy, remorse and self-reflection that saves us from ourselves. The struggle for survival, the interplay between prey and predator, does not appear to engender feelings of guilt or remorse among animals. But as human beings, we can imagine and empathize with the plight of others. It is this remorse, this capacity for empathy, which plagues many of those who return from combat. The knowledge that we have the capacity to impose indignities on other human beings is the essence of human dignity. *Non sum dignus*. When we lose this capacity for empathy, when we see the other as someone who must be "educated" to embrace our values or eliminated, we slip swiftly back into the world of animals.

The call to the moral life, which includes the isolation and anxiety that often accompanies moral responsibility, is built on the human capacity for empathy. Immanuel Kant founded his ethics upon this concept. And Kant's injunction always to "recognize that human individuals are ends, and do not use them as mere means" runs in a direct line from the Gospels.

Those who argue that religion is the product of a time of intellectual darkness ask us to forget the wisdom of the past. They offer a new faith.

Dawkins, who blames religion for stifling human curiosity and intellectual growth, encourages people to transfer their faith to "rational" belief systems to fill the hole left by the obsolescence of religious belief. "If the demise of God will leave a gap, different people will fill it in different ways," Dawkins writes. "My way includes a good dose of science, the honest and systematic endeavor to find out the truth about the real world."[11]

Hitchens is rhapsodic about the future world made possible by science and human ingenuity. He writes of the accessibility of scientific knowledge to "masses of people by easy electronic means." Science, he promises, will soon "revolutionize our concepts of research and development."[12] He adds: "Thanks to the telescope and the microscope [religion] no longer offers an explanation of anything important."[13] Dawkins uses the term *zeitgeist* to describe what he sees as ever-increasing progress, with just the occasional "set back." [14] A glorious future, brought to us by science and reason, is within reach. They have seen the future and it works. Scientific and moral progress, however, are not the same. One advances. The other does not.

"The core of the belief in progress is that human values and goals converge in parallel with our increasing knowledge," the British philosopher John Gray wrote. "The twentieth century shows the contrary. Human beings use the power of scientific knowledge to assert and defend the values and goals they already have. New technologies can be used to alleviate suffering and enhance freedom. They can, and will, also be used to wage war and strengthen tyranny. Science made possible the technologies that powered the industrial revolution. In the twentieth century, these technologies were used to implement state terror and genocide on an unprecedented scale. Ethics and politics do not advance in line with the growth of knowledge—not even in the long run." [15]

The prospects for the human race are bleak. The worse things get in human societies, the more powerful the yearning for illusion and false hope. The reality of what we face as a species is increasingly frightening. We cannot stop the destructive forces we have unleashed. We can hope only to lessen the disasters looming before us. This will require a sober, dispassionate response, one that accepts the severe limitations of humanity and gives up utopian fantasies. It will require empathy, the ability to see the world from the perspective of those outside our culture and our nation.

Dreams of fantastic miracles and collective salvation, whether through science or God, will accelerate our doom, for they permit us to ignore reality. Our survival as a species depends on accepting our narrowing possibilities, doing what we can to mitigate disaster and reaching out to the rest of the planet in ways that promote cooperation rather than conflict.

The blustering televangelists, and the atheists who rant about the evils of religion, are little more than carnival barkers. They are in show business, and those in show business know complexity does not sell. They trade clichés and insults like cartoon characters. They don masks. One wears the mask of religion, the other wears the mask of science. They banter back and forth in predictable sound bites. They promise, like all advertisers, simple and seductive dreams. This debate engages two bizarre subsets who are well suited to the television culture because of the crudeness of their arguments. One distorts the scientific theory of evolution to explain the behavior and rules for complex social, economic and political systems. The other insists that the six-day story of creation in Genesis is fact and Jesus will descend from the sky to create the kingdom of God on Earth. These antagonists each claim to have discovered an absolute truth. They trade absurdity for absurdity. They show that the danger is not religion or science. The danger is *fundamentalism itself.*

"Men seek a universal standard of human good," Reinhold Niebuhr wrote. "After painful effort they define it. The painfulness of their effort convinces them that they have discovered a genuinely universal value. To their sorrow, some of their fellow men refuse to accept the standard. Since they know the standard to be universal the recalcitrance of their fellows is proof, in their minds, of some defect in humanity of the nonconformists. Thus a rationalistic age creates a new fanaticism. The nonconformists are figuratively expelled from the human community."[16]

The new atheists, who attack a repugnant version of religion, use it to condemn all religion. They use it to deny the reality and importance of the religious impulse. They are curiously unable to comprehend those who found through their religious convictions the strength to stand up against injustice. Hitchens writes of Martin Luther King Jr. that "in no real as opposed to nominal sense, then, was he a Christian."[17] He disparages the faith of Abraham Lincoln and assures us that Dietrich Bonhoeffer, whom the Nazis put to death for resistance, was the product of a religious belief that had "mutated into an admirable but nebulous humanism."[18] He declares Gandhi an obscurantist who distorted and retarded Indian independence, and calls the Dalai Lama a medieval princeling who is the continuation of a parasitic monastic elite. All those religious figures who found the courage to live the moral life must be maligned and dismissed as not authentically religious. Their presence speaks of another kind of religion, one these atheists do not comprehend.

These attacks dismiss those—and there are millions—who found the inner fortitude through religion to fight for justice and lead lives of compassion. It seeks to invalidate the achievement of those religious figures who lost their lives in the defense of humanity. Religious leaders, such as King or Bonhoeffer, and all those who followed them, are excluded from this version of religion. The new atheists, like all fundamentalists, flee from complexity. They can cope with religion in its most primitive and abusive form. They are helpless when confronted by a faith that challenges their caricatures.

These atheists' knowledge of the Bible, as well as the Koran and other religious texts, is shallow and haphazard. They do not distinguish between religious myth and factual narrative, between a truth expressed through story or art and the truth that arises from a factual investigation into a historical event or a scientific experiment. They are blind to the underlying human truth and reality expressed through religious myth. The Bible, which they are so fond of attacking as incoherent, was never designed to be a coherent book. The word *Bible* is derived from the greek words *ta biblia*, "little books." In ancient libraries it was not a unified whole but a collection of scrolls placed in cubbyholes. These scrolls, all read separately, contained wisdom literature, moral treatises, stories, rules, aphorisms, creation myths, letters, fables, polemics, histories and poems. History, as a collection of verifiable facts, was a foreign concept to the writers of the Bible, as it was to the Greek historian Herodotus. The stories about Jesus in the Gospels were meant to convey the essence of a life and a teaching, not facts. The discrepancies in the accounts by the four Gospel writers, as well as the various versions of myths in the Hebrew Bible, including the creation myth, illustrate the indifference these writers felt to factual narrative. Those who wrote ancient texts included reportage, myth, legend, received wisdom and stories in their "historical" accounts. Readers, since the Bible came into existence, have picked and rejected what suited and did not suit the circumstances of their lives. William Blake, who understood this, referred to the Bible as "the Great Code of Art."

"If religion is essentially the inner life," wrote Wilhelm Schmidt, "it follows that it can be truly grasped only from within. But beyond a doubt, this can be better done by one in whose inward consciousness an experience of religion plays a part. There is but too much danger that the [nonbeliever] will talk of religion as a blind man might of colors, or one totally devoid of ear of a beautiful musical composition." [19]

I fear that in a period of instability and crisis, perhaps after another terrorist attack, an economic collapse or an environmental disaster, these secular and religious fundamentalists will merge to call for horrific bloodletting and apocalyptic acts of terror to save us. It does not matter if one billion Muslims are condemned as "Satan worshippers" or irrational religious fanatics. The resulting catastrophe—for them and for us—will be the same.

In *The End of Faith*, Harris, in passages that could be lifted from a sermon by a Christian fundamentalist, calls for a nuclear first strike against the Islamic world. He defends torture as a logical form of interrogation. He, like all utopians, has reduced millions of human beings and cultures he knows nothing about to primitive impediments to his vision of a better world. "What will we do if an Islamist regime, which grows dewy-eyed at the mere mention of paradise, ever acquires long-range nuclear weaponry?" Harris asks. "If history is any guide, we will not be sure about where the offending warheads are or what their state of readiness is, and so we will be unable to rely on targeted, conventional weapons to destroy them. In such a situation, the only thing likely to ensure our survival may be a nuclear first strike of our own. Needless to say, this would be an unthinkable crime—as it would kill tens of millions of innocent civilians in a single day—but it may be the only course of action available to us, given what Islamists believe." [20]

Harris again reduces a fifth of the world's population to a vast, primitive enemy. He argues that we may have to murder "tens of millions of people in a single day." His bigotry, and the bigotry of all who dehumanize others, is used to justify indiscriminate slaughter and atrocity. The people to be killed, we are told, are not distinct individuals. They do not have hopes and aspirations. They only appear human. They must be destroyed because of what they represent, what lurks beneath the surface of their human form. This dehumanization, especially by those who live in a society with the technological capacity to carry out acts of massive slaughter, is terrifying.

Our enemies have no monopoly on sin, nor have we one on virtue. We all stand in need of self-correction. We do not live in a world where we ever get to choose between pure virtue and pure vice. Human actions combine within them the moral and the immoral, no matter how pure they appear to us or to others. We are *always* like our enemy. Human virtue is *always* ambiguous.

Niebuhr captured this inclination to paint our self-interested motives as universal virtues when he wrote in *The Irony of American History* about America's response to communism during the cold war:

John Adams in his warnings to Thomas Jefferson would seem to have had a premonition of this kind of politics. "Power," he wrote, "always thinks it has a great soul and vast views beyond the comprehension of the weak; and that it is doing God's service when it is violating all His laws. Our passions, ambitions, avarice, love and resentment, etc., possess so much metaphysical subtlety and so much overpowering eloquence that they insinuate themselves into the understanding and the conscience and convert both to their party." Adams's understanding of the power of the self's passions and ambitions to corrupt the self's reason is a simple recognition of the facts of life which refute all theories, whether liberal or Marxist, about the possibility of a completely disinterested self. Adams, as every Christian understanding of man has done, nicely anticipated the Marxist theory of an "ideological taint" in reason when men reason about each other's affairs and arrive at conclusions about each other's virtues, interests and motives. The crowning irony of the Marxist theory of ideology is that it foolishly and self-righteously confined the source of this taint to economic interest and to a particular class. It was, therefore, incapable of recognizing all the corruptions of ambition and power which would creep inevitably into its paradise of innocency.[21]

Niebuhr warned that when we divide the world into darkness and light we take on the attributes of those we oppose. We adopt their language and their binary vision of good and evil, speaking also of a "new enemy" and "perpetual war." Democratic systems function because they begin from the premises that human nature is corrupt, and absolute power, as well as absolute truth, is antithetical to the common good.

"We must fight their falsehood with our truth," Reinhold Niebuhr cautioned, "but we must also fight the false-hood in our truth."[22]

This is what these secular utopians fail to do. They believe that the best human beings, defined by them as "rational" and "enlightened," should become powerful enough to dictate to the rest of the planet a new way of being. They see these "best" human beings in themselves and assume they represent the best of the nation. They fail to see their own irrationality in the irrationality of those they oppose. They have forgotten that they, too, are human. The question is never who shall rule. A democratic state begins from the assumption that most of those who gravitate toward power are mediocre and probably immoral. It assumes that we must always protect ourselves from bad government. We must be prepared for the worst leaders even as we hope for the best. And as Karl Popper wrote, this understanding leads to a new approach to power, for "it forces us to replace the question: *Who shall rule?* By the new question: *How can we so organize political institutions that bad or incompetent rulers can be prevented from doing too much damage?*"[23]

"I am inclined to think that rulers have rarely been above average, either morally or intellectually, and often below it," Popper wrote. "And I think that it is reasonable to adopt, in politics, the principle of preparing for the worst, as well as we can, though we should, of course, at the same time try to obtain the best. It appears to me madness to base all our political efforts upon the faint hope that we shall be successful in obtaining excellent, or even competent, rulers." [24]

Those who call on us to carve out a world in our own image and tame and quell "irrational" religious fanatics offer an invitation to despotism. In the name of noble ideals and universal harmony they empower the demons of self-exaltation, greed and lust for power. This utopian vision imbues human history and human nature with a fictitious linear progression toward an idealized future.

"The point is that we have almost moved on, and in a big way, since biblical times," Dawkins writes. "Slavery, which was taken for granted in the Bible and throughout most of history, was abolished in civilized countries in the nineteenth century. All civilized nations now accept what was widely denied up to the 1920s, that a woman's vote, in an election or on a jury, is the equal of a man's. In today's enlightened societies (a category that manifestly does not include, for example, Saudi Arabia), women are no longer regarded as property, as they clearly were in biblical times. Any modern legal system would have prosecuted Abraham for child abuse. And if he had actually carried through his plan to sacrifice Isaac, we would have convicted him of first-degree murder. Yet, according to the mores of his time, his conduct was entirely admirable, obeying God's commandment. Religious or not, we have all changed massively in our attitude to what is right and wrong." [25]

Dawkins argues that we are "way ahead of our counterparts in the Middle Ages, or in the time of Abraham, or even as recently as the 1920s. The whole wave keeps moving, and even the vanguard of an earlier century (T. H. Huxley is the obvious example) would find itself way behind the laggers of a later century. Of course, the advance is not a smooth incline but a meandering sawtooth. There are local and temporary setbacks such as the United States is suffering from its government in the early 2000s. But over the longer timescale, the progressive trend is unmistakable, and it will continue."[26]

Dawkins's hope that George Bush is an aberration on the road to enlightenment is naïve. It dismisses the rise of a militarized corporate state that has slowly cannibalized the democratic system and made the corporations a shadow government. The corporate state will not vanish when Bush leaves office. Dawkins applauds the taming of past evils—although human trafficking and slavery continue in Asia, Africa and Eastern Europe—and ignores new ones, such as industrial warfare and nuclear weapons, the brutality of totalitarian capitalism, globalization and looming environmental disasters. We do not march toward a rational paradise. We march toward a world where the rapacious and greedy appetites of human beings, who have overpopulated and failed to protect the planet, threaten widespread anarchy, famine, nuclear terrorism, and wars for diminishing resources. The belief that the human animal is evolving morally and will finally become reasonable is possible only when we close our eyes to the human predicament. Human beings prefer hope, even absurd hope, to truth. It makes life easier to bear. It lets us turn away from the hard choices ahead to bask in a comforting certitude that God or science will bring about our salvation.

History, as a meaningful narrative of progress shaped by human beings, is unknown in the traditions of Asia or Africa. This vision of history is a peculiar product of the Christian faith and the Enlightenment. This vision was tempered within Christianity, however, by the acknowledgment of human corruption or sin. The Enlightenment myth, which discarded the concept of sin, taught that our physical and social environment could be transformed through rational manipulation. We could advance morally as a species. This belief in rational and scientific manipulation of human beings to achieve a perfect world has consigned millions of hapless victims to persecution and death.

Human history is not a long chronicle of human advancement. It includes our cruelty, barbarism, reverses, blunders and self-inflicted disasters. History is not progressive. The ancient Greeks, like Hindus and Buddhists, saw human life and human history as cyclical. We live, they believed, in alternating stages of hope and despair, of growth and decay. This may be a more accurate understanding of human existence. To acknowledge the purposelessness of human history, to refuse to endow it with a linear march toward human perfection, is to give up the comforting idea that we are unique or greater than those who came before us. It is to accept our limitations and discard our intoxicating utopian dreams. It is to become human.

The worst tyranny in human history was carried out by utopian idealists. These idealists plunged their nations and societies into famine, war and genocide for great ideals and laudable virtues. Utopian dreams are always psychotic. They promise that we can achieve what no generation before us has achieved. They ask us to unleash, one last time, acts of horrific violence and repression to make ourselves happy. These dark visions begin with the annihilation of the other, but end with self-annihilation. In the name of beauty, progress, goodness and truth they bring death.

CHAPTER TWO

Science and Religion

Science without religion is lame, religion without
science is blind.

—Albert Einstein[1]

E instein's quest for a unified field theory explaining
subatomic structure did not undermine religious contemplation. Neither did the Big Bang or evolutionary biology.
The questions of science are not the questions of religion.
Science does not attempt, nor is it capable of, addressing the
mystery of existence, our moments of transcendence, the
moral life, love, our search for meaning and our mortality.
Science, limited to what can be proved and disproved, is a
morally neutral discipline. There are times when it protects
and advances life. There are times when it empowers those
who seek to dominate and kill. Science, like all human
endeavors, comes with good and bad, possibilities of hope
and possibilities of destruction.

Evolution is a biological theory that helps us grasp

descent, with modification, within living species. It is not a theory about economic systems, government, morality, ethics or the behavior of nations. To be sure, Darwinian evolution can give us analogies for certain aspects of human behavior. But atheists such as E.O. Wilson and Dawkins have mistaken these analogies for reality. Distorting evolutionary biology to explain how we should conduct human affairs and structure human organizations is as specious as making the Ten Commandments the basis of our legal system. The Ten Commandments—only two of which are codified into our legal system—are about lusts and violations that are largely beyond the reach of law. They were not called commandments when they first came into being. They were called "the Ten Words." Evolutionary biology was, likewise, never designed as a blueprint for all human behavior. Darwin did not set out to create an unassailable litmus test for human conduct. This misuse of evolutionary biology is part of the cult of science. It provides, like all fundamentalism, an escape from reflection and thought. It permits a retreat into artificial constructs that do not correspond to human reality. It makes the world easy to understand, quantify and direct toward the spurious goal of human perfection.

Darwinism sees our animal natures as intractable. It never attempts to argue that human beings can overcome biological limitations and create a human paradise. It infers the opposite. The belief in collective moral progress is anti-

Darwinian. The cult of science is used, like the cult of religion, to provide meaning and hope, to feed the illusion of moral superiority. Since scientific knowledge is cumulative, it lends itself to the illusion that human history and human morality are cumulative. A belief in the limitless possibilities of science, and the belief that science will save us from ourselves, has replaced, for many, faith in God.

The new atheists, angry and polemical, adopt the rhetorical style of the bigots they attack. They have failed to heed the wisdom of the Darwinian advocates, such as T. H. Huxley—the man who coined the word *agnosticism*—whom they claim to follow. They sound like the shrill anti-Darwinian campaigner Bishop Samuel Wilberforce. And it was Huxley, in words these atheists should regard carefully, who rebuked the bishop's stupidity with the words: "I asserted—and I repeat—that a man has no reason to be ashamed of having an ape for his grandfather. If there were an ancestor whom I should feel shame in recalling, it would rather be a man—a man of restless and versatile intellect—who, not content with an equivocal success in his own sphere of activity, plunges into scientific questions with which he has no real acquaintance, only to obscure them by an aimless rhetoric, and distract the attention of his hearers from the real point at issue by eloquent digressions."[2]

When Darwin published *On the Origin of Species by Means of Natural Selection, or the Preservation of Favored Races in the Struggle for Life* in 1859, he named natural selection as the mechanism that drives and defines life. Evolutionary science, however, swiftly became for many a surrogate religion. It was used to promote racism and pseudoscience, such as eugenics, a theory of biological determinism invented by Francis Galton, Darwin's first cousin. It was turned like a club on religion and used to justify exploitation and neglect of the poor and disadvantaged.

Darwin was a disciple of Thomas Malthus, whose theories about food and population helped formulate laissez-faire capitalism and Social Darwinism. And Darwin ranks human races (like the "Aryan" and the "Asiatic") in a hierarchy by their proximity to the apes. He wrote in his notebooks that competition, free trade, imperialism, racial extermination, and sexual inequality were all natural outcomes in a developed human society. Darwin included Galton's eugenic theories and Herbert Spencer's theory about the "survival of the fittest" in the 1874 second edition of *The Descent of Man*. He called *Hereditary Genius*, Galton's treatise on the biological nature of intelligence and moral character, "remarkable,"[3] and Spencer "our great philosopher."[4]

But Darwin, unlike Spencer, was not a teleological utopian. There was, for Darwin, no final goal. Darwin saw that species accrued mutations and adaptations that, over time, caused change. They could become a different species. Human beings, for example, have the ability to communicate abstract thoughts. Chimps, although they share a common ancestor with us and a primitive form of communication, do not. The six million years since our divergence from chimps have led to vast differences. Darwin refused, however, to speculate about where this was headed. He sought to explain how species accrue more useful adaptations to their world and are able to persist or how they fail to adapt and struggle to survive. He was a careful and rigorous scientist. It is impossible to infer from his research that the human species is moving toward an end point.

There are unfortunate implications in Darwin's theory of evolution. Darwin believes in the possibility of compassion and benevolence. He argues that these adaptations give one species advantage over another. In his discussion of compassion, however, he insists that sooner or later the "superior" races—those with compassion—will exterminate the "more savage" races. Compassion, he implies, does not exist, or certainly not in the same abundance, in others as it does in us. But Darwin left the championing of these implications to others such as Spencer, a utopian and a doctrinaire Malthusian. It was Spencer, not Darwin, who argued that step by step we were progressing as a species and would end with the perfect human being.

Social Darwinism bears many similarities to religious fundamentalism. It justifies the political, social and economic domination of those who are weaker or who are poor. In Social Darwinism it is nature rather than God that blesses the strong and the privileged. But the self-delusion is the same. The new atheists of the twenty-first century, while they do not endorse the hierarchy of races or espouse the crude racist doctrines of earlier Social Darwinists, continue to argue that natural selection is social selection. They continue to create moral hierarchies among human beings and use these hierarchies to sanction violence. They do this because they insist we are moving toward a final good. This is not a position supported by either human history or evolutionary biology.

Friedrich Nietzsche's biographer Curtis Cate noted Nietzsche's delight in Darwin's "calm annihilation of the fairy-tale fable of the creation of the world, as related in Genesis, and its serious attempt to view the huge span of biological evolution from a non-anthropocentric, non–man-centered point of view." He welcomed Darwin's assertion that humankind was "the product of fortuitous accidents as were any of the 'lower' species."[5] But Nietzsche also grasped how Darwin could be used to bolster the moral bankruptcy of British imperialism. He worried that Darwin would be used to justify the greed and abuse of British industrialists and imperialists. They could claim, because they were powerful, that they stood at the pinnacle of human society. Evolution, twisted into Social Darwinism, saw rapacious capitalism and callous indifference to the weak and the poor as part of the natural order. Scientific and rational utopianism could also be used to explain the necessity of imperial exploitation and repression.

"What Nietzsche did not like about Darwinism, on the other hand, was what one of Darwin's most influential propagandists, the sociologist and philosopher Herbert Spencer, had contributed: the notion of 'survival of the fittest,' " Cate wrote of Nietzsche. "While it seemed to sum up admirably the essence of Darwin's thesis, this shorthand formula in effect begged the question. Survival of the fittest, fine; but 'fittest' for what? Fittest to survive? If this was the be-all and end-all of human existence, it was not much to boast about. Indeed, in terms of logic it was something of a vicious circle, not to say a tautology. For if there was one thing that human history proved, it was that it was often those who were the least fitted to survive in a strictly physical sense—geniuses who had died prematurely, like Raphael and Giorgione, like Mozart, Schubert and Chopin, club-footed limpers like Byron and Talleyrand, or high-strung epileptics like Alexander the Great, Julius Caesar and Muhammad—who had contributed the most to human culture. In any purely utilitarian evaluation of the process of human evolution—and for Nietzsche, Spencer was the very prototype of the English utilitarian—it did not really matter what sort of human beings were produced, provided that they demonstrated their capacity to survive. Such a 'philosophy' could only end up implicitly justifying the mass perpetuation of idiots and brutes, of 'rudimentary human beings,' of *Dauermenschen* (made-to-last human beings)."[6]

E. O. Wilson, in his book *On Human Nature*, uses evolutionary biology to justify power structures such as the subjugation of women and social inequality. All behavior in society, he argues, has a genetic basis. Religious belief exists, he writes, only because it gives humans a biological advantage. Religion helps "congeal identity," provides "unquestioned membership in a group claiming great powers" and gives to human beings "a driving purpose in life compatible with [their] self-interest."[7] Wilson, while correct in assuming that many of the laws that govern animals also govern the behavior and habits of the human species, goes much further. He leaps from science to the unscientific propositions that evolution means we can, as a species, morally advance. He dreams of a day when the human race, having jettisoned religion and embraced science and reason, will be able to alter human nature and control its own destiny:

> . . . genetic evolution is about to become conscious and volitional, and usher in a new epoch in the history of life . . . The prospect of this "volitional evolution"—a species deciding what to do about its own heredity—will present the most profound intellectual and ethical choices humanity ever faced . . . humanity will be positioned godlike to take control of its own ultimate fate. It can, if it chooses, alter not just the anatomy and intelligence of the species but also the emotions and creative drive that compose the very core of human nature.[8]

Dawkins, as brilliant a scientist as Wilson, also makes the leap from science to the cult of science. He writes that the human species, unlike other animals, can transcend its biological map: "We are built as gene machines and cultured as meme machines, but we have the power to turn against our creators. We, alone on earth, can rebel against the tyranny of the selfish replicators."[9]

This leap by Wilson and Dawkins is a leap of faith. It is not Darwinian science. Darwin wrote nothing to indicate that the human species had risen above its biological composition. He argued that human morality *was* linked to the behavior of animals. The social instincts that constitute humankind's understanding of moral behavior can be found, he wrote, in monkeys, pelicans and dogs, as well as other animals: "Any animal whatever, endowed with well-marked social instincts, the parental and filial affections being here included, would inevitably acquire a moral sense or conscience, as soon as its intellectual powers had become as well developed or nearly as well developed, as in man."[10]

Wilson and Dawkins build their vision of human perfectibility out of the legitimately scientific theory that human beings are shaped by the laws of heredity and natural selection. They depart from this position when they assert that we can leave that determinism behind. There is nothing in science that implies that our genetic makeup allows us to perfect ourselves. Those who, in the name of science, claim that we can overcome our imperfect human nature create a belief system that functions like religion. It gives meaning. It gives purpose and hope. But it is a myth. It is not true. And there is nothing, when you cut through their scientific jargon, to support their absurd proposition.

Human beings are not exempt from the evolutionary laws. Those who believe in this exemption disregard human nature, human history and evolutionary biology. These atheists have twisted and perverted the theory of evolution to make it fit a utopian vision. Evolution shows us that the roots of the present are sunk deep in the past. It allows us to see how natural processes, which we can observe, explain these biological connections. But evolution is nearly useless in explaining nonbiological activities. The pseudomethodological attempt to impose the patterns observed in biological science onto the workings of human collective and personal relationships also has grave consequences. If a scientific hypothesis does not work, it is discarded. Pluralism has no place in science. Neither does the principle (so familiar from the arts, humanities and human sciences) of competing truths. Science, when set up as a model for our moral and social existence, implicitly banishes compromise and tolerance. Scientific ideas, because they can be demonstrated or disproved, are embraced or rejected on the basis of quantifiable evidence. But human relationships and social organizations interact and function effectively when they are not rigid, when they accept moral ambiguity, and when they take into account the irrational. Politics, for example, is an endeavor that concerns the channeling and managing of human drives and desires. It is only fitfully in contact with reason. This profound understanding of the irrational element in politics led Freud to write his masterpiece, *Civilization and Its Discontents*. Attempts to deny the irrational increase the potency of the irrational.

Pluralism and tolerance thrive by acknowledging the nebulous and morally ambiguous nature of politics, art, religion and human social interaction. We build a democracy by accepting that we are all tainted by prejudice, often captive to the irrational, and frequently blinded by self-interest. Human action cannot be examined and quantified as easily as elements in a science experiment. It is the result of a sophisticated interplay of internal and external forces. The human brain is a complex machine. It is able to veto the promptings of impulse and habit. It is wired, although perhaps not all the time or even most of the time, to make possible the exercise of free choice, or at least an extraordinarily large range of possible choices. It can lead us to carry out acts that are contrary to our own self-interest and self-preservation. But the human mind is always subject to the concealed impulses of the subconscious. The more sophisticated biology becomes, the less applicable the old-fashioned reductionism of those who believe in a purely rational existence.

Epigenomics, the study of DNA string, for example, illustrates that there is no rigid template for the morphological "fate" of an organism. The DNA string is a complex, highly interactive switchboard that makes possible an array of fates for an organism. These outcomes are influenced by the environment. They are affected by the way genes interact within the genome. Epigenomics confirms that DNA does not predetermine human behavior. Human genes always lay out an array of possibilities. Biology is not a prison. It has given us freedom of choice. It is not absolute freedom, and there are moments when overpowering instincts such as fear, along with what we have been taught and how we have grown up, predetermine our reactions. But a tempered freedom does exist. The moral and ethical heights human beings are capable of attaining are a testament to the reality of this tempered version of free will. They are also a testament to the glory, not the bondage, of human biology.

The extinction of our species, though tragic, would not mean the extinction of life. The human race is not at the center of creation. We are bound to the fragile ecosystems that make life possible. We can exploit and destroy these ecosystems, as we are doing, but we cannot master them. If we destroy these ecosystems, then we kill ourselves. Those who seek to transform and mutilate our environment in the name of progress are engaged in an act of self-annihilation. Those who believe human beings can be morally reformed are no less suicidal. The drive to fashion a new heaven and a new Earth through technology and science leads to wide scale human suffering and self-annihilation. This utopian vision, fed by the cult of science, served as the excuse for the Nazi and Communist sterilization programs. It was behind the genocide of Pol Pot. It was behind Hitler's "rectification of frontiers." And it is behind the mad pursuit of fossil fuels and the reckless emission of greenhouse gases. These delusions seem to elevate the deluded, especially those who are deemed to be favored by race or nature, above other forms of life. This lack of reverence, this refusal to see that we exist as an integrated whole, blinds humankind to its vulnerability, the fragility of life and human weakness. These delusions are part of a worldview that has lost touch with the sacred, a worldview that places itself and its selfish desires and dreams before the protection of life itself.

These atheists, like Christian fundamentalists, corrupt evolutionary biology. They assert that evolutionary biology implies an absolute materialism that banishes the role of religion. The Christian fundamentalists do this to discredit science and defend their absurd biblical myths. The new atheists do this to discredit religion and justify their faith in the cult of science. These atheists use science the way religious fundamentalists use religion, to arrogate to themselves moral authority over all creation, including those within their own species who are too dim to see the truth. They alone (they think) understand how to bring about collective salvation and redeem the human race.

Hitchens claims he is a former Trotskyite who saw the folly of his left-wing views and swung to embrace the neocon agenda of imperial power and preemptive war. But his shift, ideologically, was negligible. Leon Trotsky, like all totalitarian ideologues, was also an ardent believer in the radical transformation of human life, and in particular human nature, through science and social engineering. In his 1923 pamphlet *Literature and Revolution*, he predicted a world where "man will become immeasurably stronger, wiser and subtler; his body will become more harmonized, his movements more rhythmic, his voice more musical. The forms of life will become dynamically dramatic. The average human type will rise to the heights of an Aristotle, a Goethe or a Marx. And above this ridge new peaks will rise." [11]

Hitchens remains captive to the illusion that the human species can progress through reason and science. He has traded the hollow slogans of the left for the hollow slogans of the right. But he never discarded his dangerous utopian fantasies, his Enlightenment belief in collective moral progress. It does not matter if these dreams come cloaked in the rhetoric of a Trotsky or a Leo Strauss. Those who attempt to mend the flaws in the human species embrace a perverted idealism that is sadly familiar in light of all twentieth-century tyrannies. Those who believe that history is a progressive march toward human perfectibility no longer know what it is to be human. In the name of the highest virtues they sink to moral depravity. This self-delusion bedevils the modern age. It comes to us in many forms. It can be wrapped in the language of religion; atheism; a "master race"; *Liberté égalité fraternité*; the worker's paradise; the idyllic agrarian society;

the "new man"; science or reason. The jargon is varied. The dark sentiment is the same.

Joseph Conrad understood the savage capacity of Western civilization for inhuman exploitation. He saw in the Congo the barbarity and disdain for human life that resulted from faith in moral advancement. He knew humankind's violent, primeval lusts. He knew how easily human beings slip into extreme depravity. *"L'homme est un animal méchant. Sa méchanceté doit être organisée,"* he wrote. *"Le société est essentielle-ment criminelle,—ou elle n'existerait pas. C'est l'égoïsme qui sauve tout,—absolument tout,—tout ce que nous abhorrons, tout ce que nous aimons."* [12] [Man is a cruel animal. His cruelty must be organized. Society is essentially criminal,—or it wouldn't exist. It is selfishness that saves everything,—absolutely everything,—everything that we abhor, everything that we love.] Conrad rejected all formulas or schemes for the moral improvement of the human condition. He despaired of human institutions ever securing human happiness. He wrote:

International fraternity may be an object to strive for . . . but that illusion imposes by its size alone. *Franchement*, what would you think of an attempt to promote fraternity amongst people living in the same street, I don't even mention two neighboring streets? Two ends of the same street. There is already as much fraternity as there can be,—and that's very little and that very little is no good.

What does fraternity mean? Abnegation,—self-sacrifice
means something. Fraternity means nothing unless the
Cain-Abel business. That's your true fraternity. *Assez*.[13]

He bluntly told Bertrand Russell, who saw humankind's
future in the rise of international socialism, that it was "the
sort of thing to which I cannot attach any definite meaning.
I have never been able to find in any man's book or any
man's talk anything convincing enough to stand up for a
moment against my deep-seated sense of fatality governing
this man-inhabited world."[14]

Russell said of Conrad: "I felt, though I do not know
whether he would have accepted such an image, that he
thought of civilized and morally tolerable human life as a
dangerous walk on a thin crust of barely cooled lava which at
any moment might break and let the unwary sink into fiery
depths. He was very conscious of the various forms of pas-
sionate madness to which men are prone, and it was this
that gave him such a profound belief in the importance of
discipline."[15]

The cult of science promises to eradicate or reform the
tainted and morally inferior populations of the human race.
This cult resulted, in Nazi Germany, in the slaughter of
Jews, the mentally ill, gypsies, "inferior" races and homosex-
uals. It resulted in the Soviet Union's massive famines and
pogroms. And those who champion the cult of science must
make war on science. The cult always becomes absurd. This

is why, in the name of science, the regimes in Nazi Germany and the Soviet Union became scientific backwaters. Adolf Hitler sent expeditions to Tibet to find the forefathers of the Aryan race. He financed experiments to breed apes with human beings and create a race of oversized warriors. The Soviet Union attacked "Jewish" science and "bourgeois biology," leading the Soviet authorities to reject Einstein's physics and Mendel's genetics. The cult of science foists upon science an impossible task—that of transforming human nature. When science fails to achieve this goal, as it always will, science is discarded and replaced by gimmicks dressed up as science.

Science can be as inexact and intuitive as theology, philosophy and every other human endeavor. The German chemist August Kekulé fell asleep in his study after a fruitless struggle to identify the chemical structure of benzene. He dreamed of a snake eating its own tail and awoke instantly. The dream gave him, through the ancient subconscious language of symbolism, the circular structure of the benzene ring that had eluded his conscious mind. The dream may have had its basis in Kekulé's experiments, but it was the nonrational that brought him his discovery. Many physicists see "string theory"—in which the structure of the universe is made up of resonating, one-dimensional submicroscopic strings—as plausible. Yet no scientist has ever seen a string. No direct experimentation has established very firm ground for them. Cosmology routinely bases arguments on things that cannot be seen in order to explain things that can, as in the case of "dark" matter, which, it is argued, *must* exist since its effects can be seen throughout the universe. Quantum physics demolished the assumption that physical elements are governed by laws pervious to prediction and conventional analysis, meaning we cannot ever know the ultimate workings of the universe beyond the expedient of probability.

A mirror demonstrates the ultimate unknowability at the heart of nature. Consider a mirror that reflects about 95 percent of photons hitting it. The other five percent pass through the mirror. Photons, the smallest packets of light, are either reflected or pass through the mirror's surface. But there is no way of knowing which photons will be reflected and which will be absorbed.

"If we fire a series of one hundred photons at the mirror," wrote Kenneth R. Miller,

> Can we tell in advance which will be the five percent that are going to pass through? Absolutely not. All photons of a particular wavelength are identical; there is nothing to distinguish one from the other. If we rig up an experiment in which we fire a single photon at our mirror, we cannot predict in advance what will happen, no matter how precise our knowledge of the system might be. Most of the time, that photon is going to come bouncing off; but one time out of twenty, on average, it's going to go right

through the mirror. There is nothing we can do, not even in principle, to figure out when that one chance in twenty is going to come up. It means that the outcome of each individual experiment is unpredictable *in principle*.[16]

Electrons are also subject to these quantum effects. This led physicist Werner Heisenberg to formulate his "uncertainty principle." This principle states that we cannot know everything about a particle. If we can determine a particle's position, we cannot determine its momentum. We can measure momentum, but in this measurement we lose the particle's exact position. We can know a particle's momentum or its position, but we cannot know both with definitive accuracy.

"I remember discussions . . . which went through many hours till very late at night," Heisenberg wrote, "and ended almost in despair, and when at the end of the discussion I went alone for a walk in the neighboring park, I repeated to myself again and again the question: 'Can nature possibly be as absurd as it seemed to us in these atomic experiments?' "[17]

Science is *not* always directly empirical. Science is *not* governed by absolute, immutable laws. Science, and especially quantum mechanics, far from telling us we can know everything, tells us there will always be things we cannot know. No one ultimately understands. Science affirms the complexity and mystery of the universe. Science, like the religious impulse, opens us up to a world where we face mystery. There are forces in the universe that will always lie beyond the capacity of the human mind.

All cults foster a class of high priests who speak of human possibility and progress in obscure, specialized jargon. They talk of miracles. They promise a healthy, long and wonderful life, one where human suffering will be vanquished and peace and happiness will prevail. Jesus makes this possible for fundamentalists; science makes it possible for the new atheists.

These atheists have become the high priests of the cult of science. Wilson, Dawkins, Dennett and Susan Blackmore call religious beliefs a variety of "memes." Memes are defined as cultural artifacts—prototypical ideas—that invade and restructure minds in order to reproduce themselves. A meme replicates in human minds, they argue, the way genes replicate in human bodies. A word, belief, thought, religious ritual, dance, poem or any of the myriad of behaviors that are copied and reproduced in human societies—all these are memes. Although memes, unlike genes, are not identifiable physical structures, Dawkins uses the image of a virus to describe them. Religion, for Dawkins, is a meme equated with a disease, and the religiously inclined are disease-carriers.

The attempt to equate patterns of human society with the behavior of genes, while it sounds plausible, and may even be instructive in some settings, is part of the cult of science.

The genetic coding that permits the transfer of DNA-encoded units of information is fairly precise. But this model fails to work for the transfer of cultural, social, ethical and political behavior. Patterns of morality are easily reversed or erased, especially in ages of revolutionary fervor, war, anarchy, fear, social decline and despotism. Those who are schooled in identical religious texts, even within the same household, have different views of morality and ethics. Ideas do not replicate like genes. Ideas are snuffed out or forgotten, often for centuries. It is possible to transfer literal meaning. It is possible to transfer genetic information. It is possible to pass on heritable characteristics mediated by hard-and-fast rules of chemistry and physics. These rules, however, have no counterpart in the dissemination of ideas.

Ideas that prevail are not the best ideas but more often ideas backed by power. The rise of Christianity owed more to the brutality of Constantine and the Holy Roman Empire than it did its theology. Those who advocate the theory of memes ignore the role of power, repression, persecution and force in human history, as well as the inherent chaos and irrationality of human thought. Human thought cannot be treated like an object in a laboratory. There is no scientific mechanism that explains cultural evolution and cultural decline.

Those who endorse meme theory speak of "memetic engineering." This would involve the conscious manipulation of intellectual evolution by disseminating good memes and curtailing bad ones. The question of who decides which memes are good and which bad is not raised. Dennett has argued that human evolution can be shaped and directed through memetic engineering. He advocates not science but indoctrination, a new variation of thought control. The theory of memes and the notion of memetic engineering, like the idea of the "new man," is a form of magical thinking. It is not real. It has no more scientific validity than the teaching called intelligent design. Should it ever be adopted, it would result in anti-intellectualism, a war on science and democratic freedom, and a silencing of those who fail to conform.

These atheists, like religious fundamentalists, seek the imprint of science, reason and scholarship to promote utopian schemes. The most legitimate forces in modern society are not religious. They are legal and scientific. The Christian fundamentalists, although they talk about Biblical tradition, are in this regard distinctly modern. They cannot dismiss science and rely on the Bible as the infallible word of God. This day is over. Darwin obliterated it. And so they have created the elaborate pseudoscience of intelligent design to "prove" that their Biblical worldview is scientific. The secular fundamentalists, in a gross misuse of Darwin, also distort science to turn biological evolution into a methodology to perfect the human race. The use of pseudoscience is part of the atheist and the Christian fundamentalist movements. Both camps seek to give to their arguments the patina of unassailable truth and scientific legitimacy. But what they sell are myths, new forms of faith and the self-delusion that makes these fantasies possible. The Bible and Darwin, if on nothing else, agree that human nature is fixed and irredeemable.

CHAPTER THREE

The New Fundamentalism

To live is to war with the trolls.
—Henrik Ibsen, "Et Vers"[1]

Fundamentalism is a mind-set. The iconography and language it employs can be either religious or secular or both, but because it dismisses all alternative viewpoints as inferior and unworthy of consideration it is anti-thought. This is part of its attraction. It fills a human desire for self-importance, for hope and the dream of finally attaining paradise. It creates a binary world of absolutes, of good and evil. It provides a comforting emotional certitude. It is used to elevate our cultural, social and economic systems above others. It is used to justify imperial hubris, war, intolerance and repression as a regrettable necessity in the march of human progress. The fundamentalist murders, plunders and subjugates in the name of humankind's most exalted ideals. Those who oppose the fundamentalist are dismissed as savages, condemned as lesser breeds of human beings, miscreants led astray by Satan or on the wrong side of Western civilization. The nation is endowed with power and military prowess, fundamentalists argue, because God or our higher form of civilization makes us superior. It is our right to dominate and rule. The core belief systems of these secular and religious antagonists are identical. They are utopians. They will lead us out of the wilderness to the land of milk and honey.

The atheists and the religious fundamentalists speak in slogans. Atheists ridicule magic, miracles and an anthropomorphic God. They remind us that the world is not 6,000 years old, that prayer does not cure cancer, and that there is no heaven or hell. But these are not thoughts. They are self-evident tautologies. These two camps never step outside their narrow intellectual boundaries. The atheists believe they know religions' inadequacies, although they have never investigated religious thought. They delight in critiques that are, to any first year seminarian, shallow and stale. Hitchens assures us that "the unanswerable question of who . . . created the creator" has never been addressed by theologians. Theologians, he says, "have consistently failed to overcome" this conundrum.[2]

This is the declaration of an illiterate. Aquinas, along with many other theologians, addressed at length the issue of who created the creator. God, Aquinas argues, is not an entity. God is not a thing or a being. Creation is not an act of handicraft. Creation is the condition of there being something rather than nothing. Creation didn't happen long ago. Creation is a constant in human existence. It is part of life. And this is why "creationism"—the belief in a single, definitive act of invention by an anthropomorphic god—is pseudoscience and pseudotheology.[3] But stepping out of the cartoonish and childish taunting of religion to a discussion of the writings of Aquinas, Augustine, Paul Tillich, Karl Barth and Reinhold Niebuhr is beyond the capacity of these atheists. They haven't read them and they don't want to.

All fundamentalists reject intellectual investigations. They know the truth. They live wrapped in the comforting and self-deluding belief that they have nothing left to learn. Hitchens, for example, assures us that "religion spoke its last intelligible or noble or inspiring words a long time ago."[4] There is no need to read theology. Harris insists he understands the Muslim world because he has read opinion polls and passages in the Koran. These atheists, like Christian fundamentalists, maintain that one can be linguistically, culturally, historically and socially illiterate and make sweeping statements about other cultures and other traditions. This celebration of ignorance fits neatly into a world that has traded dialogue for the chanting of slogans and clichés. A passage from my debate at UCLA on May 22, 2007, with Sam Harris, moderated by the columnist Robert Scheer, captured this intellectual void.[5]

HEDGES: You dismiss this notion that somehow despair is unimportant [and insist that Muslims] react like barbarians because of the Koran. You know, if you go back and read the great philosophers on totalitarianism, on Nazi Germany, Hannah Arendt, Karl Popper, Fritz Stern's *The Politics of Cultural Despair*. They all write that what propelled the fascists forward, what propels all totalitarian movements, and I include fundamentalists, Jewish fundamentalists, Christian fundamentalists, Islamic fundamentalists, Hindu fundamentalists [is despair]. Karen Armstrong has done great work on this. What propels them forward is despair, personal and economic despair. You see this in the United States with the Weimarization of the American working class, the rise of the American oligarchy, the huge discrepancies that they are creating. You can't maintain a democracy in an oligarchic state. What is at fault in the Arab world is not Islam but scummy little dictatorships like the one run in Saudi Arabia or Hosni Mubarak in Egypt. It's the political system that keeps most people under, crushed under their heel. Egypt is a deeply repressive state, which we give $3 billion a year to. Let's also finally not forget that every time Israel sends those F-16 jets and Apache helicopters to strike refugee camps in Gaza, the fragments of those bombs have Dayton, Ohio, and other cities on them. And we are complicitous very much in the suppression and abuse and killing of innocent Muslims.

HARRIS: OK, well, let me deal with your taking your measure of the Muslim world. Happily we do not assess public opinion by having *New York Times* journalists go out and live in the Muslim world and make friends and get a vibe. I mean, this is not . . . a single well-run opinion poll would be worth a thousand years of you wandering around the Middle East.

SCHEER: Come on.

HARRIS: That's not meant to be hyperbolic.

SCHEER: Wrong, wrong, wrong.

HARRIS: Let me tell you—

SCHEER: You can't possibly believe that about polls, my God—

HARRIS: All we've got is conversations; all we've got is conversations.

SCHEER: The man has lived there for 15 years, for God's sake.

HARRIS: How many people did you ask?

SCHEER: I've done it for two hours, how long . . . go on.

HARRIS: How many people did you ask whether they supported suicide bombing? You could have lived there a long time and asked that question a lot and still not have done anything like the job that Pew did when they went into nine countries and got a random sample, insofar as that was possible of Muslims, and asked 38,000 people that question. The responses were appalling. And the responses were appalling in countries that were the most cosmopolitan and the least benighted by pre-modern standards. This is, and there has been poll after poll after poll . . . none of them support this sanguine idea of Muslim public opinion.

SCHEER: I actually studied the Pew poll carefully, and what it said was that in the face of an occupation, where the occupier is hurting your country and your people, that this is a legitimate attack because you don't have alternatives. That's what the Pew poll said.

Harris follows the line of least resistance. He does not engage in the hard and laborious work of acquiring knowledge and understanding. Self-criticism and self-reflection are a waste of time. Nuance and complexity ruins the entertainment and defeats the simple, neat solutions he offers up to cope with the world's problems. He does not deal in abstractions. He sees all people as clearly defined. The world is divided into those who embrace or reject his belief system. Those that support him are good, and forces for human progress. Those that oppose him are ignorant at best, and probably evil. He has no interest in debate, dialogue or scholarship. Complexity makes it impossible to speak in absolutes. Complexity spoils the game.

Atheists like Harris, like the Christian fundamentalists, consider themselves the vanguard. They are the chosen few. They see and know the truth. They claim, like all of the elect throughout history, to be able to carry out the will of God or give us the tools that will advance human destiny. They have been given, by their own superiority and insight, the right to impose their vision on the rest of us. This vision is as seductive as it is absurd. And the absurdity is part of its attraction. *Credo quia absurdum*—I believe because it is absurd. The belief in a world morally progressing through reason and science feeds an old fantasy human beings have long cherished about themselves. Reality cries out against the impossibility of such a vision. But reality is not an impediment to fundamentalists, lured into the warm embrace of a world devoid of intellectual constructs and a confrontation with reality. The utopian dream repeatedly overpowers the intellect because it satisfies deep emotional and psychological longings. It fosters an exalted sense of self-worth. It makes us feel safe and assured. It justifies our indiscriminate use of power. Built on a scaffolding of lies, such beliefs allow the believer to reject compassion and empathy. They eradicate individual conscience. They are hard to resist. The alternative means facing a world that will not be glorious. It means we cannot place ourselves at the center of creation and must accept that, tainted and flawed like all human beings, we will never rise to the heights of angels or create a paradise on earth. It means that we too are bound to this earth on a wheel of fire.

There were philosophers, even during the inception of the Enlightenment, who questioned the visions of a perfect, rational world. Baruch Spinoza, while conceding that human beings were distinguished from animals by their capacity for rational inquiry, also grasped that rational inquiry was usually not the engine that drove human beings to act on them. "All are not naturally conditioned to live so as to act according to the laws and rules of reason."[6]

This understanding of the power of instinct to shape us, often under the guise of reason, was expanded and amplified by Freud, who examined the array of unconscious human desires. Human will, as Spinoza and Freud saw, was always morally ambiguous. The freedom to act can result in the construction of concentration camps as often as in the safeguarding of human rights and liberty. Societies and individuals have, throughout history, ignored rational calls for altruism and mutuality and embarked on suicidal campaigns of violence and war.

The modern, industrialized state with its advanced weapons and bureaucracies has empowered killers who in a pre-modern era might have remained marginal. They have been able to organize and oversee the murder of millions. The industrial age brought with it the possibility of industrial killing. It sputtered to life in the orgy of death that was the

First World War. Machine guns, gas grenades, artillery fire, tanks, torpedoes, planes and zeppelins gave war a new sheath of technology. This continued in the Second World War, in which 72 million people, 47 million of whom were civilians, perished. The atomic bomb alone killed 140,000 people at Hiroshima. The Holocaust, with its mechanized death camps, armies of government clerks, disciplined armies and transportation systems, was the logical outcome of the scientific and technological advances begun with the industrial revolution. In the period between 1917 and 1959, more than 60 million people were killed in the Soviet Union. The growing capacity of industrialized nations to obliterate tens of thousands of people who never see their attackers signals a descent into a stygian nightmare. It has led terrorists to seek cruder versions of the apocalyptic weapons stockpiled by industrialized nations. Terrorists reach out for dirty bombs and chemical and biological agents while Washington speaks of deploying tactical nuclear weapons. This is the dark side of human progress. It is what Conrad witnessed in the Congo. It is the marriage of technological, scientific and intellectual advances with ancient, primitive lusts for violence, domination and death. It is the marriage of technological sophistication with the irrational.

"It is not the brutal SS man with his truncheon whom we cannot comprehend; we have seen his likes throughout history," writes the historian Omer Bartov. "It is the commander of a killing squad with a Ph.D. in law from a distinguished university in charge of organizing mass shootings of naked women and children whose figure frightens us. It is not the disease and famine in the ghettos, reminiscent perhaps of ancient sieges, but systematic transportation, selection, dispossession, killing, and distribution of requisitioned personal effects that leaves us uncomprehending, not for the facts but their implications for our own society and for human psychology."[7]

James Luther Adams, my ethics professor at Harvard Divinity School, spoke of the "old triumvirate of tyrants in the human soul, the libido sciendi, the libido sentiendi, and the libido dominandi" [The lust of the mind, the lust of the flesh and the lust for power]. Adams, who worked with the anti-Nazi church leader Dietrich Bonhoeffer in 1935 and 1936 in Germany, warned us that these lusts are universal and intractable. They lurk beneath the surface of the most refined cultures and civilizations. "We may call these tendencies by any name we wish," he said, "but we do not escape their destructive influence by a conspiracy of silence concerning them."[8]

The belief that science or religion can eradicate these lusts leads to the worship of human potential and human power. These lusts are woven into our genetic map. We can ameliorate them, but they are always with us; we will never ultimately defeat them. The attempt to deny the lusts within us empowers this triumvirate. They surface, unexamined and unheeded, to commit evil in the name of good. We are not saved by reason. We are not saved by religion. We are saved by turning away from projects that tempt us to become God, and by accepting our own contamination and the limitations of being human.

The belief in moral advancementment implicitly calls on us to ignore the common good and place our faith in the empowerment of the state. It teaches that everything should be dedicated to private gain. The corporate state—the engine, we are assured, of our great moral progress—instructs us on how to view the world. Corporatism is about placing our faith in unchecked corporate advancement, as well as in the neutral disciplines of science and technology. The effect on the individual in the emergent corporate state is a kind of numbing acceptance of our political, economic and social disempowerment. We give over our rights as citizens because we are taught to believe these forces will lead us to utopia. There is, as John Ralston Saul wrote, a passivity and conformity "in those areas which matter and nonconformism in those which don't."[9] We view the status quo as an unadulterated good. We are assured it is leading us to a wonderful and glorious future. We do not question. We are left to seek our individuality and our identity in the trivial and the banal.

A CNN show called *Art of Life* recently profiled the fashion designer Tom Ford. The show, as is common on television, blurred news and entertainment. It offered faux individualism through fashion. Monita Rajpal, the reporter, who spoke over shots of Ford at a lavish party held in Milan to launch his new perfume, promised the viewers "unprecedented access!"

"When I left Gucci, I went out to try and buy something to wear, and I couldn't find anything . . ." Ford said. "The quality from a lot of our competitors wasn't up to my standard, so then I started having all of my clothes made in London, where I live part of the time, on Savile Row, which was a very *dry* experience. There was really the need for something that I don't think has ever existed for men before, which is a cross between a Savile Row tailor and a fashion company."

The camera panned over floor-to-ceiling dark wood shelves, filled with white dress shirts with stiff collars. The recessed lighting highlighted the white cloth against the dark wood.

"I think the market is ready for it because he's got a totally unique product," said Dylan Jones, the editor of *GQ* magazine, as he stood next to a rack of Ford's gray suit coats. "Where he's going right, is that what he's doing, he's doing something that no one else is doing. So sort of different to what is happening in the market place in terms of style, in terms of entry points, amount of product, it's very, very clever. It's brave, but I think it'll work."

"Describe for me the difference between Tom Ford the man and Tom Ford the product," Rajpal asked Ford.

"Tom Ford the product is very confident, very strong,"

Ford answered. "Tom Ford the man is also those things, but Tom Ford the man is also very shy. And nobody ever believes that about me. Being public for me is a performance. That doesn't mean it's not genuine. But I have to get my head into the place, and I have to perform, and I have to be Tom Ford the product."

We are sold items or experiences that, we are told, will make us unique and strong and confident and authentic individuals, even as we are stripped as citizens of real authenticity and individuality. Democracy, the corporate state tells us, is the product of economics. The free market means a free people. But democracy predated the industrial revolution. Democracy was, as Saul points out, the political system that "made most of the economic events possible, not vice versa."[10] And so, in the name of freedom and progress, jobs are outsourced, benefits are cut, government assistance programs are slashed, and civil rights are curtailed. This, we are assured, is the cost of progress.

Those who hold power justify it by seeking to make it part of the natural order. Global capitalism becomes the engine that drives human progress. It leads to the highest form of civilization. Advocates for global capitalism effectively promote this faith even as they move factories from the United States to Mexico, China and the Philippines, where wages are low and workers are denied basic rights, health care and benefits. They talk of a new world order as they build a new serfdom. The atheists and Christian fundamentalists, because they serve mechanisms of power, because they refuse to deal in complexity, reduce the rage and violence of the world's dispossessed to human imperfections that can be eradicated. If the disaffected can be converted to Christianity or become endowed with reason, we will all be safe and happy. If not, we must do away with them. They do not investigate the brutality and injustice of imperial aggression, the callousness of totalitarian capitalism and the role of poverty and repression as triggers for violence and terrorism. They blame the victims.

Mohandas Gandhi, standing on the other side of this divide, understood how Western industrialized powers created glorious histories and moral crusades to obscure or justify slavery, massacres, despotism and the destruction of traditional arts, crafts and languages. He understood the lies we tell ourselves. The attack on the weak was not part of the necessary price for progress and the advance of civilization; it was part of a program of raw exploitation by unfettered capitalism. The stories used to defend this exploitation created a cult of history much like the cult of religion or the cult of science. It permitted immorality in the name of noble and virtuous ideals. These visions of an emergent world of light and universal civilization are always employed by those in power to hide their tracks. As Albert Camus wrote, "We are living in the era of premeditation and the perfect crime. Our criminals are no longer helpless children who could plead love as their excuse. On the contrary, they are adults and they have a perfect alibi: philosophy, which can be used for any purpose—even for transforming murderers into judges." [11]

"The West does not like to admit this fact about itself," wrote William Pfaff and Edmund Stillman, that it "has been capable of violence on an appalling scale, and has justified that violence as indispensable to a heroic reform of society or of mankind." The atomic bomb, napalm, phosphorus raids, and indiscriminate area bombing were American and British techniques, used in "a mission of bringing liberty to the world." The technological and scientific advances of industrialized nations made possible the conquests and the theft of natural resources in Africa, Asia and the Middle East. "To be a man of the modern West," Pfaff wrote, "is to belong to a culture of incomparable originality and power; it is also to be implicated in incomparable crimes." [12]

The human race will not be redeemed by the domination of the globe by "civilized" and "rational" people. We cannot rise to moral and intellectual levels never achieved before in human history. Those who advocate this utopia seek to become Nietzsche's new man, the Übermensch, the Superman. Übermensch, Nietzsche wrote, rejects the sentimental tenets of traditional Christian civilization. The Übermensch creates his own morality based on human instincts, drive and will. The will to power means, for Nietzsche, that the modern man has gone "beyond good and evil." The modern man spurns established, traditional religious values. He has the moral fortitude and wisdom to create his own values. This belief creates a human deity. Religion, which has failed humankind, will be banished. We will all become Übermenschen.

The absurdity of this human deity did not prevent Nietzsche from seeing where it could lead. Nietzsche warned that this new faith might, in fact, prefigure something else—a pathetic, middle-class farce. Nietzsche foresaw the deadening effects of the bourgeois lust for comfort and personal self-satisfaction. Science and technology might, instead, bring about a race of *Dauermenschen*, of Last Men. The Last Man would ignore and disdain all that went before him. The Last Man would wallow in his arrogance, ignorance and personal contentment. He would be satisfied with everything he has done. He would seek to become nothing more. He would be stagnant, incapable of growth, part of an easily manipulated crowd. The Last Man would confuse cynicism with knowledge.

"The time is coming when man will give birth to no more stars," Nietzsche wrote about the Last Man in the prologue of *Thus Spoke Zarathustra*. "Alas! The time of the most contemptible man is coming, the man who can no longer despise himself." [13]

"They are clever and know everything that has ever happened: so there is no end to their mockery." [14] The great causes of the human race lie defeated or reviled. The Last

Man endows the empty banality of his private life with universal meaning. The Last Man withdraws from larger concerns, indulging "their little pleasure for the day, and their little pleasure for the night." [15]

Nietzsche attacked the pretensions and dishonesty of rational consciousness. He wrote: "Do not deceive yourselves: what constitutes the chief characteristic of modern souls and modern books is not the lying, but the innocence which is part and parcel of their intellectual dishonesty . . . Our cultured men of today, our 'good' men do not lie, that is true; but it does not redound to their honour. The real lie, the genuine, determined honest lie (on whose value you can listen to Plato) would prove too tough and strong an article of them by a long way; it would be asking them to do what people have been forbidden to ask them to do, to open their eyes to their own selves, and to learn to distinguish between 'true' and 'false' in their own selves." [16]

The consumer culture, as Nietzsche feared, has created tens of millions of Last Men. Atheists such as Harris and Hitchens exemplify these Last Men. They are tiresome epicures. They promote, as Chalmers Johnson says, a "consumerist Sparta." It is the poor and desperate who fight our wars. The impoverished, often without legal rights, do the dirty work for a bloated, self-absorbed oligarchy and its compliant middle-class managers. Curtis White in *The Middle Mind* argues that most Americans *are* aware of the brutality and injustice used to maintain the excesses of their consumer society and empire. He suspects they do not care. They don't want to see what is done in their name. They do not want to look at the rows of flag-draped coffins or the horribly maimed bodies and faces of veterans who return home or the hundreds of thousands we have killed in Iraq. It is too upsetting. They do not want to read about the nation's growing legions of underemployed and poor, or the child laborers in sweat shops who make our clothing and our shoes. Government and media censorship—increasingly common since the attacks of 2001—are appreciated. Most prefer to be entertained.

Those who promote the new atheists' faith in reason and science offer an escape from moral responsibility and civic engagement. They express the dreams and desires of a morally stunted middle class. They promote, under a scientific veneer, the selfish lusts of the consumer society and the deadening provincialism of the petite bourgeoisie. Dawkins, in an example of this pedestrian vision, draws up his own list of commandments to replace the Biblical injunctions. He advises people to enjoy their sex lives as long as they don't harm anyone else. He calls on parents not to indoctrinate their children but to evaluate evidence. His are hollow, liberal platitudes that casually deny the seductive lusts of violence, evil and abuse—lusts the biblical writers who wrote the commandments understood and feared. These atheists are suburban mutations. They are products of a moral and political landscape corrupted by too much television, rampant waste, unchecked self-indulgence, wealth, too little contemplation, the physical destruction of community and a loss of the sacred. They tell us we are good. They tell us we will get better. And they warn us not to get in the way of progress.

Neither Christian fundamentalists nor the new atheists question the rape and pillaging of the country by corporations and the dismantling of our democracy. Why not? Because they are locked in a non-reality-based belief system in which things are seen as getting better when in fact they are getting worse. They can be morally and politically irresponsible because they are bedazzled by magic, miracles and utopian dreams. This utopia will arrive, we are assured, if we will remain politically passive. We must let those in power do their work. These utopian ideologies are anesthetics. They turn us into sheep who are manipulated and led astray.

Evil, for the Christian fundamentalists and the atheists, is not something within them but an external force to be vanquished. It must be conquered and defeated. This may take violence, even massive acts of violence, but if it leads to a better world, this violence is justified. They have been anointed by reason or God to do battle with this terrible evil. But once evil is seen as being only external, once some human beings are proclaimed more moral than others, repression and murder becomes a regrettable necessity to improve the world. Those infected with the "vice" of evil have to be controlled or exterminated.

Dawkins sees no moral worth in religious faith, just as Christian fundamentalists see no moral worth in those who do not accept Jesus as their personal lord and savior. The millions of human beings who over the ages struggled to live lives of compassion and fought for justice under a religious or a secular banner are blithely erased from moral consideration. It no longer matters what people do with their lives, but what they believe. Dawkins, like Christian zealots, reduces the world to a binary formula of good and evil. Religion is a force of darkness. Reason and science are forces of light. He, like the religious fundamentalists he despises, views the world through this childish lens. He sees the ethnopolitical conflict in Northern Ireland, for example, as the fault of religion. The conflict, he assures us, would end if the religious beliefs of the warring factions evaporated. The terms he uses to describe the conflict, however, illustrate his ignorance of its complexity. When writing of Northern Ireland, he speaks of "loyalist" and "nationalist" as "euphemisms" for Protestant and Catholic, respectively. He does not recognize the difference between a loyalist and a unionist or a nationalist and a republican. But simplicity is a benefit when you are determined to paint wars, whether in Ireland or the Middle East, as caused by religion. Such thinking reduces the world to a monochromatic color scheme. The banishment of one nonconformist shade will suddenly solve the insoluble.

It is impossible to formulate a moral code out of reason

and science. As the realm of fact rather than value, science is notoriously unable to generate a basis for moral behavior. Neither science nor reason calls on us to love our neighbor as ourselves, to forgive our enemies, or to sacrifice for the weak, the infirm and the poor. Utilitarian notions of human behavior eschew acts of beneficence. The language of religion—the call to respect life as created in God's image— is a call to an ethic that goes beyond the utilitarian. It honors the sacred. It is not irrational, but it is also not rational. Perhaps it is best described as nonrational, for it allows believers to remain in a world that is real while holding up an ideal and an ethic that cannot be scientifically examined. This is the basis for the spiritual dimension to human existence. This religious impulse allows us to transcend what Flaubert said was our "mania for conclusions," a mania he described as "one of humanity's most useless and sterile drives." [17] Faith is not in conflict with reason. Faith does not conflict with scientific truth, unless faith claims to *express* a scientific truth. Faith can neither be affirmed nor denied by scientific, historical or philosophical truth. And this faith can separate the rational world from the powerful nonrational experiences and emotions—love would be one—that infuse and give meaning to our lives.

We live in a universe indifferent to our fate. We are seduced by myths that assure us that the world revolves around us, that fate or the gods or destiny have given us a unique and singular role in the cosmos. It is hard to reject these myths and face the bleakness of human existence. It is more comforting and reassuring to have faith in our collective moral advancement as a species, to believe that we are heading toward something great and wondrous. The bitter reality of existence and the bondage of human nature, however, are real. These myths are not. All those who tempt us to play God turn us away from the real world to flirt with our own annihilation.

CHAPTER FOUR

Self-Delusion

> If we should perish, the ruthlessness of the foe
> would be only the secondary cause of the disaster.
> The primary cause would be that the strength of a
> giant nation was directed by eyes too blind to see all
> the hazards of the struggle; and the blindness would
> be induced not by some accident of nature or history
> but by hatred and vainglory.
>
> —Reinhold Niebuhr,
> *The Irony of American History* [1]

Most moral thinkers—from Socrates to Christ to Francis of Assisi—eschewed the written word. Once things are written down they become codified. Passages of sacred or philosophical texts are twisted, reinterpreted and rewritten to accommodate those in power, bolster the unassailability of religious institutions, and silence dissidents. Writing freezes speech. George Steiner calls this "the decay into writing." This is especially dangerous for ethical and moral philosophy, since, where philosophy and prescription see only virtue or vice, in reality human actions combine the two to different degrees. Our choices in life are never between the purely moral and immoral. We must choose between the immoral and the more immoral. Moral laws, rules and edicts, when codified and blindly obeyed, lead to a suspension of conscience.

All ethics begin with religion. We must determine what moral laws to accept and reject. We must distinguish between real and false prophets. This is not the religion of authority, magic and taboo. This is religion built on the ethics of personal responsibility and freedom of conscience. Where rigid, formal obedience to law allows the adherent to avoid ethical choice, the truly moral life grapples with the inscrutable call to do what is right, to reach out to those who are reviled, labeled outcasts or enemies, and to practice compassion and tolerance, even at the cost of self-annihilation. And all ethical action begins with an acknowledgment of our own sin and moral ambiguity. Those religious figures who build their ethical systems out of their own limitations, their acceptance of sin as a reality, confuse these atheists.

King, Hitchens assures us, was "a profound humanist . . . his legacy has very little to do with his professed theology."[2] King alludes to the Bible, Hitchens asserts, for convenience and dramatic effect, as "the 'Good Book' was the only point of reference that everybody had in common."[3] But the examples King gave from the book of Moses were, "fortunately for all of us, metaphors and allegories,"[4] Hitchens adds. "At no point did Dr. King—who was once photographed in a bookstore waiting calmly for a physician while the knife of a maniac was sticking straight out of his chest—even hint that those who injured and reviled him were to be threatened with any revenge or punishment, in this world or the next . . . In no real as opposed to nominal sense, then, was he a Christian."[5] Hitchens dismisses King's religious upbringing, his theological education and his religious convictions. He seeks to claim the civil rights leader as his own. The hijacking of King for the cause of humanism mirrors the attempts by Christian fundamentalists to also claim King as their own. They present themselves, like those fighting for their rights in the 1960s, as embattled and besieged, small islands of goodness and righteousness hemmed in by powerful forces of injustice. And they too evoke King as part of their heritage. "Give us somebody. Give us somebody like Martin—what poor whites called Dr. King," Rod Parsley, the head of the World Harvest Church and prominent Christian Right leader, said in Washington. "Give us somebody like Martin to stand over Washington Mall again, and say, 'God hasten that day when all God's children, black men and white men, Jews and gentiles, Protestants and Catholics, may join hands and sing in the words of that old Negro spiritual, "Free at last, free at last, thank

God Almighty, we're free at last" ' ".[6] The attempt to own King, who was neither an atheist nor a Christian fundamentalist, is an effort to ignore the religious tradition he actually represented and recruit him for a tradition (either religious or secular) he would have rejected.

Totalitarian societies persecute and silence prophets. Democratic societies tolerate them at their fringes. Artists, writers, theologians and philosophers, all those who explore the fundamental questions of meaning and existence, of doubt and mystery, all those who listen to their inner authority, must defy the crowd. They usually keep their distance from institutionalized religion. They seek to preserve and portray that which lies beyond the realm of scientific or historical fact, but which also constitutes part of our collective existence. This is why so much of great religious writing comes to us in the form of stories. It is through stories, the stories told to us and the stories we tell others, that we find meaning.

The story of the crucified Christ, rejected by the mob, abandoned by his friends, and legally condemned, speaks of the fate of many who choose a life of conscience. Those who silenced Jesus represent the powerful in all human societies. When Jesus attacks the chief priests, scribes, lawyers, Pharisees, Sadducees and other "blind guides," he is attacking an authoritarianism as endemic to Christianity as to all institutions and ideologies. The story of Christ's death is a reminder that what is sacred in life always appears to us in flesh and blood. It is not found in abstract ideas or utopian schemes for human perfectibility. The moment the writers of the gospels began to set down the words of Jesus they began to kill the message. The central doctrine of Christianity—something perhaps all great religious thinkers have believed—is, as the Dominican theologian Herbert McCabe said, if you don't love you're dead, and if you do, they'll kill you.

Samuel Beckett detested religious and metaphysical beliefs that championed the myth of human progress. He ridiculed the false hope of changing the world, reforming human nature and controlling human destiny. These beliefs, he knew, ignored human reality. They gave the world, as well as our own lives, a coherence it did not possess. He tore apart, often with biting humor, the absurdity of our dreams of advancement.

The title character of Beckett's 1951 novel *Molloy* is a former tramp, living in his mother's room. "My life, my life, now I speak of it as of something over, now as of a joke which still goes on," Molloy ponders, "and it is neither, for at the same time it is over and it goes on, and is there any tense for that?"[7]

Beckett's play *Endgame* is set in a bare interior with grey light. Hamm is a blind tyrant confined to a wheelchair. Clov is his haggard servant. They wind up an alarm clock and listen to it ring. When it stops Clov says: "The end is terrific." Hamm replies: "I prefer the middle." Hamm and Clov treat the sound as if it has a beginning, a middle and an end. For Beckett, life, like the ringing of the clock, has a steady monotony. There is no beginning, middle or end. The structure imposed by Hamm and Clov on the sound of the alarm is the structure we impose on our lives and on human history. It is a fiction. It is a product of the forlorn human hope that we are moving toward some culmination. Beckett saw that we live in a perpetual middle. The characters in Beckett's works always exist on the margins of society. Only there, denied the protective coverings of class, social position, money and physical strength, do they gain insight into the frailty and absurdity of being human.

Molloy knows that the ordered precision of a life laid out in résumés, film plots, novels or biographies are literary devices. They are lies. Molloy is after something else. He knows the lie of creating a coherent, linear narrative: "That is to say, I could say it, but I won't say it, yes, I could say it easily, because it wouldn't be true."[8] He reminds us that he uses phrases such as "then I thought" or "then I said" because he is following a human convention, one that consistently alters reality to give it a fictional coherence, order, narrative and meaning. And whenever he uses these conventions, he says that he is "merely complying with the convention that demands you either lie or hold your peace."[9]

The stories we construct about ourselves give us the illusion of a fixed identity, but to Molloy, and to Beckett, these stories are not true. "If I go on long enough calling that my life I'll end up believing it," Molloy says. "It's the principle of advertising." [10] The truth of existence is ultimately impossible to understand. Life is too confusing. Molloy intends, as far as possible, to face this confusion:

> All I know is what the words know, and the dead things, and that makes a handsome little sum, with a beginning, a middle and an end as in the well-built phrase and the long sonata of the dead. And truly it little matters what I say, this or that or any other thing. Saying is inventing. Wrong, very rightly wrong. You invent nothing, you think you are inventing, you think you are escaping, and all you do is stammer out your lesson, the remains of a pensum one day got by heart and long forgotten, life without tears, as it is wept. To hell with it anyway. [11]

"For in fact what is man in nature?" Pascal asked in *Pensées* number 72. "A Nothing in comparison to the Infinite, an All in comparison with the Nothing, a mean between nothing and everything. Since he is infinitely removed from comprehending the extremes, the ends of things; and their beginnings are hopelessly hidden from him in an impenetrable secret; he is equally incapable of seeing the Nothing from which he was made, and the Infinite in which he is swallowed up." [12]

The new atheists respond to this human hunger for *telos*, a belief that all that has gone before us is leading us somewhere. This desire for moral advancement has repeatedly corrupted religious and secular ideologies. We want to believe that human suffering and deprivation is meaningful, that it has a purpose and that our lives make sense. This yearning for *telos* creates imaginary narratives of moral and historical progress. It feeds into the faith that human society will finally become reasonable and work collectively for the common good. It is a way to ward off the awful fact that things often do not get better, that they often get worse, and that the irrational urges of human nature will never be conquered.

The myth of collective moral progress and *telos* allows us to dismiss looming disasters. It offers an escape route. It hides from us the fact that we control little, even within our own lives, that our most important decisions are often made by others, or motivated by unconscious, conditioned forces we cannot articulate. Human societies can never achieve what we have failed as distinct individuals to achieve: complete consciousness and control of the world around us. Søren Kierkegaard, in the introduction to *On Authority and Revelation*, wrote of this human desire for progressive, linear movement and tidy endings:

> . . . the lives of . . . men go on in such a way that they have indeed premises for living but reach no conclusions— quite like this stirring age which has set in movement many premises but also reached no conclusion. Such a

man's life goes on till death comes and puts an end to life, but without bringing with it an end in the sense of a conclusion. For it is one thing that a life is over, and a different thing that a life is finished by reaching a conclusion.[13]

Those who believe they know how to bring about a conclusion to life seek to eradicate all other schemes for human perfection. These competing visions, in their eyes, pollute society, lead people astray, and stymie the ultimate possibility of human happiness. The new atheists, like all true believers, want these competing visions destroyed. They call for the physical annihilation of those they brand irrational, reminding us that "Muslims are utterly deranged by their religious faith."[14] They demand the abolishment of religious institutions, although Dennett suggests that religious traditions be permitted to leave a few artifacts behind as curiosities: "What, then," Dennett writes, "of all the glories of our religious tradition? They should certainly be preserved, as should the languages, arts, the costumes, the rituals, the monuments. Zoos are now more or less seen as second-class havens for endangered species, but at least they are havens, and what they preserve is irreplaceable. The same is true of complex memes [religion] and their phenotypic expressions [churches] . . ."[15]

Dennett continues: "My own spirit recoils from a God Who is He or She in the same way my heart sinks when I see a lion pacing neurotically back and forth in a small zoo cage.

I know, I know, the lion is beautiful but dangerous; if you let the lion roam free, it would kill me; safety demands that it be put in a cage. Safety demands that religions be put in cages too—when absolutely necessary." [16]

Dawkins condemns competing faiths as blind faiths. He dismisses those who follow these faiths as heretics—albeit heretics from his religion. Those who find meaning in religion lack the capacity to question and doubt, an irony lost on Dawkins, who suffers from the same disorder. He insists that the existence or nonexistence of God is a scientific hypothesis. It is open to rational demonstration. He ridicules the concept of a personal God with anthropomorphic attributes. He asks how this God can speak to billions of people simultaneously. He excoriates the belief that dietary laws or tithes or appropriate dress or rituals or degree of faith determines what will happen to a person in life. He attacks a belief in magic. He belittles absurd beliefs, but he proposes an absurdist system of his own, placing faith for our salvation in human reason. This singular attack on religion allows these atheists to avoid confronting moral and ethical dilemmas that stand outside of scientific testability. This is not to deny that many institutional religions champion absurd behaviors and beliefs. Science, has, in some celebrated instances, shown how many of these beliefs—such as the six-day creation account or the 6,000-year-old earth—are not true. But the new-atheist attack on absurd forms of religion is also used to avoid confronting the core and most important issues taken up by religious thought.

Dawkins asserts the accidental nature of existence. This is a claim beyond the ability of science to test or prove. When asked why human beings are here, he explains: "We won the lottery!" What he elides, cleverly, is that we have won billions and billions of lotteries to exist and trillions that fell together inside and outside our solar system so we could be on planet Earth. Dawkins has said he is open to the "multiverse" theory, in which, by some accounts up to 10^{550}—an unimaginable number—of other universes exist. There is no way to test this idea. It is, in its own way, a form of mysticism. If we did win the lottery, as Dawkins claims, we won it not only here on Earth but in this multiplicity of universes. I do not dispute Dawkins on this point. What he says may be true. But Dawkins, like most human beings, slips with this belief into realms of mystery.

We are, as Augustine wrote, both similar to and different from animals. We, like animals, have an innate drive to survive. We will, especially when we feel endangered, often turn to violence to eradicate forces bent on our destruction. I encountered this primal human capacity for violence in the some one dozen wars I covered for two decades as a foreign correspondent in Central America, Africa, the Middle East and the Balkans. It is a tragic reality of human nature. Discussions of pacifism during the siege of Sarajevo, where I was stationed for *The New York Times*, would have evoked gales of laughter and ridicule. Sarajevo was encircled by besieging Serb forces. The Serbs used their Soviet-era tanks as artillery pieces on the heights above the city to lob 90 mm shells below. They rained mortars and rockets on Sarajevo, dropping up to 2,000 shells a day on an area twice the size of Central Park. The city was peppered with sniper fire. There were an average of four to five dead and two dozen wounded a day. The dozens of razed villages, foundations of houses blasted into disuse, and mass graves in the Drina Valley were an ominous reminder of our fate should the Serbs break through the patchwork of barricades and trench systems that surrounded Sarajevo. Those in the city, who lacked running water, heat and often food, picked up weapons to stave off the Serb forces. There was little debate. Few of us would act differently.

But at the same time the use of violence to protect the city empowered the worst elements in Sarajevo, the gangsters and criminals, the thugs who had access to weapons and a penchant for violence. There was nothing romantic about it. Violence is a dirty and venal business, one that permits gratuitous acts of killing and turns the moral order upside down. In the squalid enclave of Sarajevo the criminals and killers became kings, surrounded by bodyguards, rich from the loot they stole and endowed with the godlike power to give and take life. This human capacity for violence and the moral filth it empowers lurks below the surface of our ordered societies. We can all, given the right circumstances, embrace it. We can all become beasts.

When we are desperately afraid, when chaos and disorder envelop life, when the world is reduced to a bitter struggle to get enough to eat and stay alive, the fragile, "civilized" veneer that coats our existence in times of prosperity, order and safety vanishes. The coherent, rational self disintegrates, we sink swiftly into the depravity the atheists see as the result of religious fanaticism. Few of us are immune. Most of us can be thrust, as Varlam Shalamov wrote in *Kolyma Tales*, his book on his years in a Soviet labor camp, into a life where "cold, hunger, and sleeplessness rendered any friendship impossible" and where we grimly understand "the falseness of the belief that friendship could be tempered by mercy and tragedy. For friendship to be friendship, its foundations had to be laid before living conditions reached that last border beyond which no human emotion was left to man— only mistrust, rage, and lies." [17]

"All human emotions—love, friendship, envy, concern for one's fellow man, compassion, longing for fame, honesty— had left us with the flesh that had melted from our bodies during their long fasts," [18] Shalamov wrote.

Primo Levi in *Survival in Auschwitz* chronicled a moral disintegration as bleak as that portrayed in *Kolyma Tales*. He argued that those who carried out selfless acts of compassion in Auschwitz were the first to perish. Only the worst survived. Levi described the psychological death of emaciated and dehumanized victims that preceded death itself. He wrote that inmates who cared for others wasted away faster and died. The few able to carry out isolated acts of kindness were inmates who, through luck, cunning or bribery, held privileged positions within the camps. They worked in a kitchen or a laboratory. They had the good fortune, on occasion, to be human. To the mass of concentration camp victims, however, human solidarity was a luxury they could not afford. To make morality one's deepest commitment usually meant death.

Levi echoes Shalamov's bitter conclusion—it is possible to crush millions of human beings, possible to crush our capacity to be human. We can all be reduced to barbarity. We can all forsake what is moral, what makes us human, for what is expedient. We can place our physical survival above moral considerations. Those groups that fared best in the camps, the criminal gangs with their effete male paramours and skill for theft and murder, or the tight solidarity of clannish communities, such as the Greeks in Auschwitz, endured at the expense of others. They were predators. Those around them were prey. The camps were always dominated by the most brutal inmates. Their savagery reflected the savagery of their guards. As Wolfgang Sofsky puts it,

> This was not a *Leidensgemeinschaft*—there was no community of suffering. The laws of the jungle prevailed in the daily struggle for survival . . . Frequently, the only way to

survive was at the expense of others. One prisoner's death was another's bread . . . Solidarity is based on the principle of mutual aid and sharing. But where there is nothing to share, except at the cost of common destruction and doom, solidarity lacks a material basis . . . Absolute power is based on a cleverly devised system of classification and collaboration, gradation of power and privilege . . . [It] thrusts individuals into a condition where what is ultimately decisive is the right of the stronger.[19]

Levi found the true image of humanity clawing for survival in Chaim Rumkowski, the Nazi collaborator and autocratic leader of the Jewish ghetto in Łódź. He was a Jew who sold out his fellow Jews for privilege and power, although he, too, was finally consumed by the Holocaust. "We are all mirrored in Rumkowski," Levi wrote. "His ambiguity is ours, it is our second nature, we hybrids molded from clay and spirit. His fever is ours, the fever of Western civilization, that 'descends into hell with trumpets and drums,' and its miserable adornments are the distorting image of our symbols of social prestige." We, like Rumkowski, "are dazzled by power and prestige as to forget our essential fragility. Willingly or not, we come to terms with power, forgetting that we are all in the ghetto, that the ghetto is walled in, that outside the ghetto reign the lords of death, and that close by the train is waiting."[20]

The Soviet gulags and the Nazi death camps exposed our

fragility. They were the natural culmination of science, technology and bureaucratic organization. The tools of slaughter change. The lust to give and destroy life does not. The urge to suspend conscience and subsume our inner life in the crowd reaches back to the dawn of human society. We seek to become masters of the universe. We, like Phaeton—the mortal son of the sun god Helios, who convinced his father to let him drive the chariot of the sun across the heavens—want unlimited power. But Phaeton's horses, feeling their reins held by a weaker, mortal hand, ran wildly off course. They dipped close to Earth, threatening to consume it in flames. Zeus, to save Earth, unleashed a thunderbolt that destroyed Phaeton. All those who dream, like Phaeton, of achieving divine power and glory, who attempt to set the heavens ablaze with their own magnificence, flirt with self-destruction. And as human ingenuity has advanced, as our tools of apocalyptic destruction have been rendered perfect in nuclear weapons, we, like Phaeton, gamble with the obliteration of the human race.

Human history is steeped in blood. Millions died at the hands of imperialist powers in Africa. The genocide of Native Americans, the genocide of the Armenians by the Turks, the Nanking massacre, during which tens and perhaps hundreds of thousands of Chinese were slaughtered by Japanese troops, and the extermination campaigns of Hitler, Stalin and Mao speak to our incessant capacity for evil. These cycles of killing are part of human existence. They are ageless. All were justified by high ideals and all set loose human depravity.

"Man has improved in competence, knowledge, and manners," William Pfaff wrote in *The Bullet's Song*, "He eats with a fork, uses the computers he has invented to spare him myriad boring tasks, and conducts his wars, when he can, in a way that allows him to avoid the distress of a direct encounter with the pain he inflicts on his victims. This is a form of progress from the axe-wielding and pelt-wearing human past. Western man also today assumes that gadgetry and industry will continue to leap forward in near-geometric progressions. He is beckoned by technology toward a future in which human consciousness is superseded by a more accommodating virtual reality, and invited by economists to a seamless global marketplace that creates ruinous disruptions in the short term, allegedly to provide universal happiness in the long term. Where all this will really end, only God would know, should He (She) still exist."[21]

We can grasp the immense divide between the infinite reach of the cosmos and our mortality and insignificance. We know we are limited and finite. This finiteness and smallness disturbs us. This awareness of human insignificance can lead us toward mysticism, toward a desire to merge with the universe. But it can also see us universalize ourselves, and seek meaning in a collective utopian vision that exalts and enlarges our lives. This universal desire to be more than human lies at the core of the ideologies of these atheists as well as the Christian Right.

"What makes mankind tragic is not that they are victims of nature," Joseph Conrad wrote in a letter in 1897; "it is that they are conscious of it. To be part of the animal kingdom under the conditions of this earth is very well—but as soon as you know of your slavery, the pain, the anger, the strife, the tragedy begins."[22]

Augustine identified this lust to enlarge ourselves as the cause of original sin. This lust constantly beckons humankind to attempt to become divine through wealth, power, fame, social prestige or a life of sensual gratification. We can also submerge our lives in collectives, into classes, ethnic groups, corporations or nations, seeking power and identity through the crowd.

The more we submerge our conscience into the will of the collective, the more power we appear to have, for suddenly we have a combined capacity to act and shape events. Utopian visions, when adopted by a nation or an armed group, swiftly become grandiose and terrifying. The voices of prudence and reason are shouted down by the intoxicated mob. The crowd, deluded by feelings of power and self-importance, turns to force and violence in the attempt to make their visions real. Those who merge the self with the crowd surrender freedom. The crowd or the nation now defines them. They find through the crowd personal anonymity and collective power. All that benefits the nation or the group becomes a universal good. All that threatens the nation or the group becomes an absolute evil.

Augustine did not have an exalted view of human institutions or government. Human societies, he wrote, are built on the blood of Cain. They are secured by strife. Human beings will never build a just society or a utopia. Coercion is the law of nations. The use of violence always has unintended consequences, as the war in Iraq illustrates, and utopian visions, backed by force, are all fated to end in criminality.

The founding myth of the United States tells its citizens that it is the duty of the nation to bring enlightenment to the rest of humanity. And an entire historical narrative has been created to perpetuate this myth. The United States of Andrew Jackson or George Washington is not the United States of Frederick Douglass or Sitting Bull. But we present our history from the perspective of the winners, from those in power. The first English settlers in Massachusetts Bay seized Pequot Indian land. They believed that as Christians they were anointed by God to control and subjugate this land. The seizures were resisted, and the skirmishes with the Pequot escalated into war. The killing of Indians soon became demanded by God. The Puritans cited one of the Psalms, which reads, "Ask of me, and I shall give thee, the heathen for thine inheritance, and the uttermost parts of the Earth for thy possession," to justify the burning of villages and mass murder. Cotton Mather said after the English set fire to a Pequot village, killing numerous women and children, that "it was supposed that no less than 600 Pequot souls were brought down to hell that day." To read the Pequot's version of this history, if it existed, would be a window into our own savagery.

The Mexican War, its butcheries and atrocities described in the memoirs of Ulysses S. Grant, as well as the process of westward expansion, enshrined the doctrine of Manifest Destiny, the right to impose power over the continent because of Providence. The United States invaded Cuba in 1898 to "liberate" the Cubans, and then went to war in the Philippines shortly after, as President William McKinley put it, "to civilize and Christianize" the Filipino people. The effort to quell the uprising that followed in the wake of the occupation of the Philippines left at least 600,000 Filipinos dead. Elihu Root, the secretary of war, proclaimed at the time: "The American soldier is different from all other soldiers of all other countries since the war began. He is the advance guard of liberty and justice, of law and order, and of peace and happiness." The ideals flaunted to justify the wars in Central America in the 1930s, and similarly in Vietnam and Iraq, are part of the long continuum of these self-delusions.

The messianic beliefs exemplified by the Puritans gained a new and deadlier momentum with each military triumph— or what we saw as triumphs—and with our growing military, industrial and economic power. But our failure to judge the limits of our power has resulted in terrible blunders, first in Vietnam and later in Iraq. The inability to listen to the stories of those we dominate and crush has left us deaf and dumb. The atheists and the Christian radicals, who cling to this warped vision of our goodness, nobility and self-appointed role as the saviors of civilization, urge us forward into imperial projects that are as foolish as they are suicidal.

CHAPTER FIVE

The Myth of Moral Progress

The idea of progress is compounded of many elements. It is particularly important to consider one element of which modern culture is itself completely oblivious. The idea of progress is possible only upon the ground of a Christian culture. It is a secularized version of Biblical apocalypse and of the Hebraic sense of a meaningful history, in contrast to the meaninglessness history of the Greeks. But since the Christian doctrine of the sinfulness of man is eliminated, a complicating factor in the Christian philosophy is removed and the way is open for simple interpretations of history, which relate historical process as closely as possible to biological process and which fail to do justice either to the unique freedom of man or the dæmonic misuse which he may make of that freedom.

—Reinhold Niebuhr[1]

The Enlightenment faith in moral advancement through science, reason and rationality should have ended with the First World War. Europeans, many of whom enthusiastically greeted the war, participated between 1914 and 1918 in collective suicide. This new industrial warfare, so massive in its scale, so unrelenting in its slaughter and so absurd in its reasoning, was often beyond the realm of imagination. It left eight and a half million soldiers dead, another six million maimed and took the lives of 10 million civilians. And it was followed two decades later by the Second World War, which saw 60 million people slaughtered, two-thirds of whom were civilians. Since the end of the Second World War, the military historian John Keegan estimates, another 50 million people have died in various conflicts.

There were many, after the First World War, who turned with ferocity against the Enlightenment faith in human reason and the possibility of human perfectibility. The dark visions of Fyodor Dostoevsky, Leo Tolstoy, Herman Melville, Thomas Hardy, Joseph Conrad and Friedrich Nietzsche found modern expression in the work of Sigmund Freud, James Joyce, Marcel Proust, Franz Kafka, D.H. Lawrence, Elias Canetti, Thomas Mann and Samuel Beckett, along with atonal and dissonant composers such as Arnold Schoenberg and painters such as Otto Dix, George Grosz, Henri Matisse and Pablo Picasso. The suffering and mass slaughter of the Second World War informed the contemporary Japanese dance form Butoh. Butoh dancers are often naked, covered in thick white paint. Their movements are torturously slow, their bodies and faces grotesquely contorted. They are shadows rising up from the horror and annihilation of Hiroshima and Nagasaki. The belief in human moral advancement, these artists saw, was absurd.

The First World War illustrated that human societies were not only often governed by the irrational, but contained subliminal longings for self-destruction, violence and death. Science and technology not only did nothing to stem these longings but empowered them. Knowledge did not set us free. Knowledge, as the biblical myth about the expulsion of Adam and Eve from the Garden of Eden illustrated, is morally neutral. It empowers good and evil. Science, the last century has shown us, has served the darkest and most violent projects of humankind.

The artists and philosophers who tore apart the myth of the Enlightenment rarely fell back on traditional religious language. But what they rediscovered for the secular age was the concept of original sin. Human beings were attracted to death as powerfully as they were to life. The human race liked to destroy, not only objects, but also other human beings. And few people, seduced by war, caught up in the intoxication of the moment and the clamor of the crowd, were immune.

Freud feared these urges. He repeatedly called for their containment. He warned in *Civilization and Its Discontents*, a work that eerily foresaw the coming mass slaughter of the Second World War, that if we could not regulate or control these urges human beings would, as the Stoics predicted, consume themselves in a vast conflagration. The future of the human race depended on blunting what he called our desire for Thanatos, the urge for death. This desire for Thanatos leads us to seek the annihilation first of others and finally of ourselves. The lusts for death and destruction are not external. They lurk in all human beings. They cannot be eradicated. All of human history, Freud wrote, was a battle between the *Thanatos*, or the death instinct, and *Eros*, the instinct to preserve, conserve and protect life. And Freud, for this reason, was pessimistic about ever eradicating war. Human beings, he wrote, "are not gentle creatures who want to be loved, and who at the most can defend themselves if they are attacked; they are, on the contrary, creatures among whose instinctual endowments is to be reckoned a powerful share of aggressiveness. As a result, their neighbor is for them not only a potential helper or sexual object, but also someone who tempts them to satisfy their aggressiveness on him, to exploit his capacity for work without compensation, to use him sexually without consent, to seize his possessions, to humiliate him, to cause him pain, to torture and kill him."[2]

We live in a permanent state of war. *Homo homini lupus*, Plautus wrote: man is a wolf to man. This state of war can be tamed and restricted by social and political institutions. It can be transferred to the ballot box, the law court or the sporting arena, but the urges seek release. These urges, when permitted to express themselves without social and political restraint, create a Hobbesian dystopia, as anyone who has been to war can confirm.

Freud cherished the constraints of a structured society, naming the family, religious authorities, the police, government and the courts, as the outside forces that hold our darker instincts at bay. He saw that the innate inclination to aggression meant that civilized society was very fragile. It was always threatened with disintegration. He warned that our instinctual lusts were stronger than our reasonable interests. The tension between the human desire to gratify these instinctual urges constantly clashed with the duty to abide by the social code. This tension created what Freud called our modern neuroses. Individuals who violated the rules suffered feelings of guilt. Those constrained by society not to act on these urges suffered anxiety and frustration. Torment and pain would always, Freud wrote, be part of life in an ordered society.

The breakdown of social and political control allows these lusts to reign. Our first inclination, Freud noted, is not to love one another as brothers or sisters. The war in Bosnia, with rampaging Serb militias, rape, torture centers, concentration camps, razed villages and mass executions, was one of numerous recent illustrations of Freud's accurate appraisal of human nature. At best, Freud knew, we can learn to live with, regulate and control our lusts, which will always result in tension, guilt, anxiety and inner conflicts. The burden of civilization is worth it.

The myth of collective moral progress feeds the aggressive instincts Freud feared. If we see ourselves as the culmination of a long, historical process toward perfectibility, rather than a tragic reflection of what went before, then we are likely to think the ends justify the means. And as fervently as Freud worked to sound the alarm bells, secular utopians rose during his lifetime on the European stage with new schemes for human perfection. Fascists and communists combined violent, revolutionary fervor with the Christian millenarian dream of a heaven on earth. They adopted the pseudoscientific doctrine that it was possible to have complete knowledge and complete mastery of the human species. It was that fusion of utopian violence and industrial and bureaucratic power that marked the birth of totalitarianism.

"Even when power is acquired by peaceful means (as was Hitler's, unlike Mussolini's or Lenin's), the idea of creating a new society of new men and of solving all problems once and for all through an inevitable revolution always remains the basis of totalitarian societies," Tzvetan Todorov wrote. "People can subscribe to the cult of science without being millenarists and without approving the use of violence (many of today's technocrats would fit this category); others may be revolutionaries without subscribing to the cult of science (and a whole group of early twentieth-century poets who called for cataclysm belong to this category). But only when the three strands of violence, millenarism, and the cult of science come together can we talk of totalitarianism proper."[3]

These totalitarians were aided by the well-meaning but naïve pacifists who appeared in large numbers throughout Europe and the United States following the First World War. The pacifists argued that human beings could be educated and molded to reject war and live in universal harmony. These pacifists, while not succumbing to the disease of militarism, were just as deluded as the militarists were by a utopian belief in human perfectibility. They failed to build an ethic from the stark limitations of human nature. In the ensuing crisis and war they became ineffectual and impotent. These pacifists rejected all acts of violence, even those that could have stopped a resurgent Nazi Germany. They kept their hands clean. This was moral abdication. They, too, divided the world into "us" and "them," those who were pure and those who were impure. They, too, sought to convert others to their higher moral state. And by their passivity they aided the forces they hoped to defeat.

The steadfast refusal by American pacifists to accept the need for force to defeat totalitarianism in the 1930s led the theologian Reinhold Niebuhr, who argued that the rise of fascism in Europe had to be countered by just such force, to break with liberal humanists. He attacked pacifism as "simply a version of Christian perfectionism."

In his essay "Why the Christian Church Is Not Pacifist,"

Niebuhr wrote that "if we believe that if Britain had only been fortunate enough to have produced 30 percent instead of two percent of conscientious objectors to military service, Hitler's heart would have been softened and he would not have dared attack Poland, we hold a faith which no historic reality justifies."[4] Niebuhr continued:

> Yet most modern forms of Christian pacifism are heretical. Presumably inspired by the Christian Gospel, they have really absorbed the Renaissance faith in the goodness of man, rejected the Christian doctrine of original sin as an outmoded bit of pessimism, have reinterpreted the Cross so that it is made to stand for the absurd idea that perfect love is guaranteed a simple victory over the world, and have rejected all other profound elements of the Christian Gospel . . . This form of pacifism is not only heretical when judged by the standards of the total Gospel. It is equally heretical when judged by the facts of human existence. There are no historical realities which remotely conform to it. It is important to recognize this lack of conformity to the facts of experience as a criterion of heresy.[5]

Pacifism, in times of war, falls swiftly out of favor—indeed it is often branded as a form of treason—but the central myth championed by the pacifists, the myth of human advancement, remains the dominant ideology. Pacifists, although they do not fuel the lust for violence, keep alive the myth that the human species can attain a state of moral perfection. This myth feeds the aggressiveness and cruelty of those who demand the use of violence to cleanse the world, to borrow a phrase from George W. Bush, of "the evildoers." The danger is not pacifism or militarism. It is the poisonous belief in human perfectibility and the failure to accept our own sinfulness, our own limitations and moral corruption. This belief in our innate goodness becomes dangerous in a crisis, a moment when human beings feel threatened. It enlarges our capacity for aggression, violence and mass slaughter.

Our innate aggressiveness, as Freud wrote, "waits for some provocation or puts itself at the service of some other purpose, whose goal might also have been reached by milder measures. In circumstances that are favorable to it, when the mental counterforces which ordinarily inhibit it are out of action, it also manifests itself spontaneously and reveals man as a savage beast to whom consideration toward his own kind is something alien."[6]

It is fear, ignorance, a lack of introspection, and the illusion that we can create a harmonious world that leads us to sanction the immoral, to embrace Kant's "radical evil." This radical evil colors the ideology of the atheists and Christian fundamentalists. Kant defined as "a radical evil" all acts of morality that are used as masks for unadulterated expressions of self-love. He declared this kind of evil as "radical" because it completely twists the basis of moral teachings to defend immorality. It is the worst form of self-deception. It provides a moral façade for terror and murder.

"Given that even failed states now possess potentially disruptive technology," Harris writes, "we can no longer afford to live side by side with malign dictatorships or with the armies of ignorance massing across the oceans . . . It appears that one of the most urgent tasks we now face in the developed world is to find some way of facilitating the emergence of civil societies everywhere else . . . It seems all but certain that some form of benign dictatorship will generally be necessary to bridge the gap. But benignity is the key—and if it cannot emerge from within a state, it must be imposed from without. The means of such imposition are necessarily crude: they amount to economic isolation, military intervention (whether open or covert), or some combination of both. While this may seem an exceedingly arrogant doctrine to espouse, it appears we have no alternatives. We cannot wait for weapons of mass destruction to dribble out of the former Soviet Union—to pick only one horrible possibility—and into the hands of fanatics."[7]

Hitchens also advocates the self-defeating concept of perpetual war and military occupation to bring about a world ruled by reason and virtue. These positions regurgitate the defense of nineteenth-century European colonialism. Atheists such as Harris and Hitchens promote violence and force to make us safe, to turn foreign cultures into carbon copies of our own, and to make possible their perverted ideal of human advancement.

"Is George Bush on a Christian crusade in Iraq and Afghanistan?' Hitchens asked when I debated him in San Francisco. "Obviously not, obviously not. Anyone who's studied what's happening in either of those countries [Iraq and Afghanistan] now knows that the whole of American policy—and, by the way, a lot of your own future, ladies and gentlemen—is staked on the hope that federal secular democrats can emerge from this terrible combat, and we can protect them and offer them help while they do so. We know that they're there—I've met them, and I love them— they're our friends. Every member of the 82nd Airborne Division could be a snake-handling Congregationalist for all I know, but these men and women, though you sneer and jeer at them, and snigger when you hear applause and excuses for suicide bombers, and you have to live with the shame of having done that—these people are guarding you while you sleep. Whether you know it or not. And they're also creating space for secularism to emerge. And you better hope they're successful."

War opens a Pandora's Box of new horrors, new disasters, increased suffering and dilemmas. It becomes its own culture. It alters reality through massive acts of violence. Saddam Hussein was a tyrant, but the utopian project of the Bush administration to remake Iraq by force has created a hell that rivals the mass killing carried out by Hussein, including the genocidal campaign against the Kurds and the Shiites. Violence as an instrument of change alters landscapes so radically that it creates a new reality often as bloody as the one it attempted to halt.

The American policy in Iraq before the war was one of containment through sanctions. It was working, not dramatically, not with the speed Iraqi opponents sought, but it had the benefit of being grounded in the real and the possible. The Iraqi military was a shadow of what it was before the 1991 Gulf War. The regime was withering. Saddam's oldest son and heir-apparent, Uday, had been crippled in an assassination attempt. Saddam brooded in his palaces and wrote bizarre romance novels. Time and patience would have worked to undo his regime. This was a policy built on the possible. It accepted our own limitations as an imperial power.

Utopian visions of a restructured Middle East, however, blinded the Bush administration and many of their supporters, including many liberal interventionists, to the endemic factionalism in Iraq and difficulty of occupation. They believed their utopian visions. They ignored the reality of Iraq. And because of their folly and blindness, their failure to work within the confines of reality, hundreds of thousands are dead, and Iraq no longer exists as a unified country.

The experiment that was Iraq, the cobbling together of

disparate and antagonistic patches of the Ottoman Empire by the victorious powers in the wake of the First World War, belongs to the history books. It will never come back. The Kurds have set up a de facto state in the north, the Shiites control most of the south, and the center of the country is a battleground. There are two million Iraqis who have fled their homes and are internally displaced. Another two million have left the country, most for Syria and Jordan, which now host the largest number of refugees per capita of any country on Earth. An Oxfam report estimates that one in three Iraqis are in need of emergency aid, but the chaos and violence are so widespread that assistance is impossible. Iraq is in a state of anarchy. The American occupation forces are one more source of terror tossed into the cauldron of suicide bombings, mercenary armies, militias, massive explosions, ambushes, kidnappings and mass executions—but wait until we leave.

It was not supposed to turn out like this. The war was sold by holding out visions of a democratic Iraq, visions peddled by the White House, fatuous pundits, a compliant media, and secular and religious fundamentalists who bought into the myth of American goodness and human advancement through violence They assured us the war would be a cakewalk. We would be greeted as liberators. Democracy would seep out over the borders of Iraq to usher in a new Middle East. Now, struggling to salvage their own credibility, they blame the debacle on poor planning and mismanagement by the Bush administration. But the fault lay in these utopian delusions.

There are probably about 10,000 Arabists in the United States—people who have lived for prolonged periods in the Middle East and speak Arabic. At the inception of the war you could not have rounded up more than about a dozen who thought this was a good idea. And this includes all the Arabists in the State Department, the Pentagon and the intelligence community. Anyone who had spent significant time in Iraq knew this would not work. The war was not doomed because Donald Rumsfeld and Paul Wolfowitz did not do sufficient planning for the occupation. The plan to reshape Iraq in an American image never had a chance. Even a cursory knowledge of Iraqi history and politics would have made this apparent.

The disbanding of the Iraqi army; the ham-fisted attempt to install the crook and, it now turns out, Iranian spy Ahmed Chalabi in power; the firing of all Baathist public officials, including university professors, primary school teachers, nurses and doctors; the failure to secure Baghdad and the vast Iraqi weapons depots from looters; allowing heavily armed American units to blast their way through densely populated neighborhoods, resulting in massive and indiscriminate violence—all turned out to be the insurgency's most potent recruiting tools. These blunders ensured a swift descent into chaos. But Iraq would not have held together even if we had been spared the gross incompetence of the Bush administration. It was doomed from the start.

The dismemberment of Iraq will unleash a mad scramble for dwindling resources that has the potential to draw in neighboring states. The Kurds, like the Shiites and the Sunnis, know that if they do not get their hands on oil they cannot survive. But Turkey, Syria and Iran have no intention of allowing the Kurds to create a viable enclave. A functioning Kurdistan in northern Iraq will accelerate the rebellion by the repressed Kurdish minorities in these countries. The Kurds, the orphans of the twentieth century, who have been repeatedly sold out by every ally they ever had, including the United States, will be crushed. The possibility that Iraq will become a Shiite state, run by clerics allied with Iran, terrifies the Arab world. Turkey, as well as Saudi Arabia, the United States and Israel, would most likely keep the conflict going by arming Sunni militias. This anarchy could end with foreign forces, including Iran and Turkey, dismembering Iraq. No matter what happens, many, many Iraqis are going to die. And it is our fault.

The neoconservatives—and the liberal interventionists, who still serve as the neo-cons' useful idiots—have learned nothing. They advocate the doctrine of preemptive war, a doctrine that the post–Second World War Nuremberg Laws define as a criminal "war of aggression." They talk about hitting Iran and maybe even Pakistan with air strikes. Strikes on Iran could trigger a wider, regional conflict. Such an action has the potential of drawing Israel into war—especially if Iran retaliates by hitting Israel.

The occupation of Iraq, along with Afghanistan, has furthered the spread of failed states. It has increased authoritarianism, savage violence, instability and anarchy. It has swelled the ranks of our real enemies—the Islamic terrorists—and opened up voids of lawlessness where they can operate and plot against us. It has nearly scuttled the art of diplomacy. It has given us an outlaw state creating more outlaw states. It has empowered Iran, as well as Russia and China, which sit on the sidelines gleefully watching our self-immolation. This is what George W. Bush and all the "reluctant hawks" who supported him have bequeathed us. They bequeathed this to us because they turned away from the real and the possible to believe that American firepower could shape the world in our own image, in our own utopia.

What is terrifying is not that the architects and numerous apologists of the Iraq war have learned nothing, but that they may not yet be finished. The United States is becoming a militaristic state, dismantling its democratic freedoms and gutting its social services in the name of national security. The rise of militarism is a familiar path taken by collapsing states. Militarism arrests social decay. It shoves it underground, where it cannot be challenged by critics and social movements. The failure to confront the oil peak, for example, means that catastrophe will descend swiftly and with an unexpected fury on the United States as supplies decline.

This is a failure of leadership, caused by the blindness of a corporate state that seeks not the common good but maximum profit.

In *A Study of History*, the historian Arnold Toynbee wrote that the construction of the Egyptian pyramids, built by the pharaohs to celebrate their immortality and the eternal power of Egyptian civilization, only furthered Egypt's decline because of the forced labor and slavery used to erect the grand monuments. The failed imperialist project in Iraq, along with the maintenance of a costly military machine and the arms industry that feeds off the American state, has likewise begun to take its toll. The United States is dependent on other countries, particularly those in the Middle East, for its natural resources. It is hostage to foreign states, which control the country's mounting debt. Its infrastructure is crumbling, its social services are in decline, and its educational system is in shambles. It is rotting from the inside out. And in the midst of this decline, our secular and religious fundamentalists hold our society up as the paragon of human possibility and goodness.

"One of the most pathetic aspects of human history is that every civilization expresses itself most pretentiously, compounds its partial and universal values most convincingly, and claims immortality for its finite existence at the very moment when the decay which leads to death has already begun,"[8] Reinhold Niebuhr wrote.

No ethical stance, no matter how pure it appears, is moral

if it is not based on the reality of human limitations. Those that launch crusades offer beautiful visions of liberation, freedom and democracy. But the impossibility of these utopian dreams turns these projects for human advancement, as we see in Iraq, into justifications for atrocity. Realism, as John Gray writes, "requires a discipline of thought that may be too austere for a culture that prizes psychological comfort above anything else, and it is a reasonable question whether Western liberal societies are capable of the moral effort that is involved in setting aside hopes of world-transformation."[9] But it is realism and human limitations we must acknowledge and respect if we are to survive as a nation and finally as a species.

CHAPTER SIX

Humiliation and Revenge

... people appeared who began devising ways of bringing men together again, so that each individual, without ceasing to prize himself above all others, might not thwart any other, so that all might live in harmony. Wars were waged for the sake of this notion. All the belligerents believed at the same time that science, wisdom, and the instinct of self-preservation would eventually compel men to unite in a rational and harmonious society, and therefore, to speed up the process in the meantime, "the wise" strove with all expedition to destroy "the unwise" and those who failed to grasp their ideas, so they might not hinder its triumph.[1]

—Fyodor Dostoevsky

We are at war with Islam," Sam Harris writes in his book *The End of Faith*. "It may not serve our immediate foreign policy objectives for our political leaders to openly acknowledge this fact, but it is unambiguously so. It is not merely that we are at war with an otherwise peaceful religion that has been 'hijacked' by extremists. We are at war with precisely the vision of life that is prescribed to all Muslims in the Koran, and further elaborated in the literature of the hadith, which recounts the sayings and teachings of the Prophet."[2]

Harris wrote his book as a response to the 2001 attacks on the World Trade Center and the Pentagon. He expresses feelings common to those threatened by catastrophic violence and collective humiliation. He is afraid. Harris justifies all methods, no matter how violent or cruel, so he can again feel safe under American domination.

He nurtures the illusion that security can be restored. This worldview ignores the subtle and complex historical and social forces, including our own complicity in the Middle East, that contributed to the attacks and ensure new ones. It defines all who threaten us as evil and gives those who feel threatened a clear, discernible identity.

Collective humiliation is a potent tool in the hands of those who wage war. The Serbian ethnic cleansing campaigns in the former Yugoslavia in the 1990s sought their moral justification in distant and often mythic humiliations suffered by the Serbs, especially the 1396 defeat of Serbian forces by the Ottoman Turks at the Field of Blackbirds in the province of Kosovo. The 600-year-old defeat bore no relation to the experiences of modern Serbia, especially since the

Ottomans were fighting feudal clans and tribes, many of whom had no affiliation with the Serbian Orthodox Church. But the mythic tale of the defeat, and the alleged treachery of the Muslims in the battle, figured prominently in windy discussions by common soldiers on the front lines in Bosnia during the war. It was at a ceremony commemorating the anniversary of the battle that Slobodan Milošević, playing to the anger of the Serbs in the crowd, found the psychological tool that would propel him to power. He promised vengeance.

The collective humiliation and the rage it produced obliterated self-reflection and self-criticism. It fed acts of aggression against Muslims. The images on the evening news in Belgrade of Serbian victims, as well as the alleged atrocities by the Muslims in Bosnia or Kosovo, were used to justify the wanton attacks by Serbs, most of them against unarmed Bosnian Muslims. The images on Serbian television were frequently intertwined with old footage from the Second World War, when the Croatian fascist Ustaše state carried out massacres and ran notorious death camps, including Jasenovac. The Ustaše had been responsible for the murder of hundreds of thousands of Serbs. This historical event allowed the Serbs of the 1990s to see themselves as victims, although Serbian forces carried out nearly all of the atrocities during the war in Bosnia and later Kosovo. Serbs insisted throughout the war that *they* were aggrieved and violated.

This sense of collective humiliation infected the populace in all of the conflicts I covered as a foreign correspondent. Israelis, with a sophistry worthy of the Serbs, would justify the repression and abuse of Palestinians in the name of the Holocaust. The United States invaded and occupied Iraq in the name of the 2001 terrorist attacks, although Iraq had nothing to do with the attack. This powerful, epidemic psychosis is not rational. Arabs become equated with Nazis. The Muslims in Bosnia become fused with Ottoman Turks. The United States sees Iraqis as al-Qaeda. Violence is sanctioned to vanquish an abstraction and crush an absolute evil. Those targeted are almost irrelevant.

"We can, in fact, speak of a worldwide epidemic of violence aimed at massive destruction in the service of various visions of purification and renewal," the psychiatrist Robert Jay Lifton wrote in *The Nation* in 2003. "In particular, we are experiencing what could be called an apocalyptic face-off between Islamist forces, overtly visionary in their willingness to kill and die for their religion, and American forces claiming to be restrained and reasonable but no less visionary in their projection of a cleansing war-making and military power. Both sides are energized by versions of intense idealism; both see themselves as embarked on a mission of combating evil in order to redeem and renew the world; and both are ready to release untold levels of violence to achieve that purpose." [3]

Lifton blames the rise of what he calls "the American

apocalyptic entity" on a constellation of forces that feed the "superpower syndrome." The country's sense of omnipotence and invulnerability was shattered by the terrorist attacks. In the eyes of those affected by this syndrome, the nation not only has a right to revenge the humiliation caused by the attacks but, because of its unique moral standing, a duty to dictate terms of existence to the rest of the world.

"We know from history that collective humiliation can be a goad to various kinds of aggressive behavior—as has been true of [Osama] bin Laden and al-Qaeda," Lifton writes. "It was also true of the Nazis. Nazi doctors told me of indelible scenes, which they either witnessed as young children or were told about by their fathers, of German soldiers returning home defeated after World War I. These beaten men, many of them wounded, engendered feelings of pathos, loss and embarrassment, all amid national misery and threatened revolution. Such scenes, associated with strong feelings of humiliation, were seized upon by the Nazis to the point where one could say that Hitler rose to power on the promise of avenging them."[4]

The attacks on the Pentagon and the twin towers led to "a determination to restore, or even extend, the boundaries of a superpower-dominated world," Lifton wrote, and "integral to superpower syndrome are its menacing nuclear stockpiles and their world-destroying capacity."[5]

War in Afghanistan and Iraq becomes a way to undo what has been done to us through reciprocal violence. The wars require a twisted logic, not only because they are waged against people who had nothing to do with the 2001 attacks, but also because they are counterproductive, since these wars feed the rage of the terrorists the nation seeks to defeat. The only effective way to fight terrorism is to isolate terrorists within their own societies. This was largely accomplished after the 2001 attacks. The United States garnered the sympathy of much of the world, including the Muslim world, after the attacks. To have built on this sympathy, to have turned the hunt for Osama bin Laden and his band of followers over to intelligence agencies instead of militarizing the problem, would have made the nation more secure. But such a response would not have allowed the country to engage in public and spectacular wars of aggression to compensate for our collective humiliation.

That sense of humiliation, ironically, is also the driving force behind al-Qaeda. Osama bin Laden uses it to justify terror. He cites the Sykes-Picot Agreement, which led to the carving up of the Ottoman Empire, as the beginning of Arab degradation. He attacks the agreement for dismembering the Ottoman Empire and dividing the Muslim world into "fragments."

Robert Pape in *Dying to Win: The Strategic Logic of Suicide Terrorism*, found that most suicide bombers are members of communities that feel humiliated by genuine or perceived occupation. Almost every major suicide-terrorist campaign—

over 95 percent—carried out attacks to drive out an occupying power. This was true in Lebanon, Sri Lanka, Chechnya, Kashmir, as well as Israel and the Palestinian territories. The large number of Saudis among the 9/11 hijackers appears to support this finding. Many Saudis, including bin Laden, view the presence of American soldiers and military bases in Saudi Arabia as an occupation of Muslim land.

Pape found that suicide bombers see violence as the way to change the public opinion of occupying powers like Israel and the United States. They hope to make the occupiers suffer, as they have, from acts of reciprocal collective humiliation. Many of these terrorists come from middle-class and wealthy backgrounds. They are often well educated. The driving force behind terror is not poverty—although this is often a great spur to suicidal rage—but rather the collective sense of national and religious humiliation. That sense is most painful to affluent members of a society. They are freed from the struggle for daily subsistence and can devote energy to avenging real and perceived injustices. They view themselves as natural leaders.

Peter Bergen and *Los Angeles Times* researcher Swait Pandey in 2005 looked at five of the most spectacular anti-Western terrorist attacks, including the 2001 attacks in New York and Washington. Of the 75 Islamist terrorists involved in these five attacks, 53 percent had attended or graduated from college. Only nine had gone to madrassas, the strict Koranic schools often denounced by many as breeding grounds for terror.

Terrorists support acts of indiscriminate violence not because of direct, personal affronts to their dignity, but more often for lofty, abstract ideas of national, ethnic or religious pride, with the goal of a utopian, harmonious world purged of evil. The longer the United States occupies Afghanistan and Iraq, the more these feelings of collective humiliation are aggravated, the greater the number of jihadists willing to attack American targets. The strident support of some of the new atheists for a worldwide war against "Islamofascism" is a public relations bonanza and potent recruiting tool for Islamic terrorists. It fuels the collective humiliation and rage we should be trying to thwart.

In a 2005 interview in *The American Conservative*, Pape said: "Since 1990, the United States has stationed tens of thousands of ground troops on the Arabian Peninsula, and that is the main mobilization appeal of Osama bin Laden and al-Qaeda. People who make the argument that it is a good thing to have them attacking us over there are missing that suicide terrorism is not a supply-limited phenomenon where there are just a few hundred around the world willing to do it because they are religious fanatics. It is a demand-driven phenomenon. That is, it is driven by the presence of foreign forces on the territory that the terrorists view as their homeland. The operation in Iraq has stimulated suicide terrorism and has given suicide terrorism a new lease on life."[6]

The United States has undertaken an undefined, amorphous war on terror, a war without limits. This war has no clear definition of victory, unless victory means the death or capture of every terrorist on earth—an impossibility. It is a frightening death spiral. It feeds on itself.

"Behind such planning and manipulation can lie dreams and fantasies hardly less apocalyptic or world-purifying than those of al-Qaeda's leaders, or of Aum Shinrikyo's guru," Lifton writes. "For instance, former Director of Central Intelligence James Woolsey, a close associate of Donald Rumsfeld and Deputy Secretary of Defense Paul Wolfowitz in the Pentagon, spoke of the war against terrorism as a fourth world war (the third being the cold war between the United States and the Soviet Union). In addressing a group of college students, he declared, 'This Fourth World War, I think, will last considerably longer than either World Wars I or II did for us. Hopefully not the full four-plus decades of the cold war.'"

The effort to purify the world is self-defeating. The United States, as Lifton states, "becomes a Sisyphus with bombs, able to set off explosions but unable to cope with its own burden, unable to roll its heavy stone to the top of the hill in Hades."[7] Those who cling to the myth of collective moral progress, who believe in a progressive view of history, who insist that the world can be controlled and shaped by us, are the most susceptible to the notion of violence as antidote. Terrorist strikes, however, do not fit into a vision of a human journey toward a magical utopia. The more uncertainty, fear and reality impinge on the vision of the utopians, the more strident, absolutist and aggressive they become in calling for the eradication of evil.

Harris, Hitchens, Dawkins and Dennett know nothing about the Middle East. They do not speak Arabic. They have never studied Islam. This ignorance does not prevent them, however, from denouncing Islam and the danger posed by the Muslim world. They costume their fear and desire for revenge as a war of ideas, a "clash of civilizations," a noble "crusade" against the pernicious force of religion. And in this clash only one belief system has any validity—their own. Once religion is banished we will all be safe.

"More generally (and this applies to Christianity no less than to Islam), what is really pernicious is the practice of teaching children that faith is a virtue," writes Richard Dawkins in The God Delusion. "Faith is an evil precisely because it requires no justification and brooks no argument. Teaching children that unquestioned faith is a virtue primes them—given certain other ingredients that are not hard to come by—to grow up into potentially lethal weapons for future jihads or crusades. Immunized against fear by the promise of a martyr's paradise, the authentic faith-head deserves a high place in the history of armaments, alongside the longbow, the warhorse, the tank and the cluster bomb. If children were taught to question and think through their beliefs, instead of being taught the superior virtue of faith without question, it is a good bet that there would be no suicide bombers."[8]

The Koran is emphatic about the rights of other religions to practice their own beliefs. It unequivocally condemns attacks on civilians as a violation of Islam. It states that suicide, of any type, is an abomination. The tactic of suicide bombing, equated by many of the new atheists with Islam, did not arise from the Muslim world. This kind of terror, in fact, has its roots in radical Western ideologies, especially Leninism, not religion. And it was the Tamil Tigers, a Marxist group that draws its support from the Hindu families of the Tamil regions of Sri Lanka, which invented the suicide vest for their May 1991 suicide assassination of Rajiv Gandhi.

Suicide bombing is what you do when you do not have artillery or planes or missiles and you want to create maximum terror for an occupying power. It was used by secular anarchists in the nineteenth and early twentieth centuries. They bequeathed to us the first version of the car bomb: a horse-drawn wagon laden with explosives that was ignited on September 16, 1920, on Wall Street. The attack was carried out by Mario Buda, an Italian immigrant, in protest over the arrest of the anarchists Sacco and Vanzetti. It left 40 people dead and wounded more than 200.

Suicide bombing was adopted later by Hezbollah, al-Qaeda and Hamas. But even in the Middle East, suicide bombing is not restricted to Muslims. In Lebanon during the suicide attacks in the 1980s against French, American and Israeli targets, only eight suicide bombings were carried out by Islamic fundamentalists. Twenty-seven were the work of communists and socialists. Three were carried out by Christians.

The vast majority of the billion Muslims on this planet—only 20 percent of whom are Arab—detest the violence done in the name of their religion. They look at the Pat Robertsons or Franklin Grahams, who demonize Muslims in the name of Christianity, with the same horror with which we look at Osama bin Laden or the leaders of Hezbollah. The Palestinian resistance movement took on a radical Islamic coloring only in the 1990s, when conditions in Gaza and the West Bank deteriorated and thrust people into profound hopelessness, despair, poverty and humiliation—conditions similar to those that are slowly empowering the radical Christian Right in our own country. Before that, the Palestinian movement was decidedly secular.

The refusal to examine Islamic culture and traditions, the sordid dehumanization of Muslims, and the utter disregard for the intellectual traditions and culture of one of the world's great civilizations are characteristic of those who disdain self-reflection and intellectual inquiry. Confronting this complexity requires work and study rather than a retreat into slogans and clichés. And enlightened, tolerant civilizations have flourished outside the orbit of the United States and Europe.

The ruins of the ancient Mughal capital, Fatehpur Sikri, lie about 100 miles south of Delhi. The capital was constructed by the emperor Akbar the Great at the end of the sixteenth century. The emperor's court was filled with philosophers, mystics and religious scholars, including Sunni, Sufi and Shiite Muslims, Hindu followers of Shiva and Vishnu, as well as atheists, Christians, Jains, Jews, Buddhists and Zoroastrians. They debated ethics and belief. Akbar was one of the world's great champions of religious dialogue and tolerance. He forbade any person to be discriminated against on the basis of belief and declared that everyone was free to follow any religion. This took place as the Inquisition was at its height in Spain and Portugal, and as Giordano Bruno was being burnt at the stake in Rome's Campo dei Fiori.

Tolerance, as well as religious and political plurality, is not exclusive to Western culture. The Judeo-Christian tradition was born and came to life in the Middle East. Its intellectual and religious beliefs were cultivated and formed in cities such as Jerusalem, Antioch, Alexandria and Constantinople. Many of the greatest tenets of Western civilization, as is true with Islam and Buddhism, are Eastern in origin. Our respect for the rule of law and freedom of expression, as well as printing, paper, the book, the translation and dissemination of the classical Greek philosophers, algebra, geometry and universities were given to us by the Islamic world. One of the first law codes was invented by the ancient Babylonian ruler Hammurabi, in what is now Iraq. One of the first known legal protections of basic freedoms and equality was promulgated in the third century B.C. by the Buddhist Indian emperor Ashoka. And, unlike Aristotle, he insisted on equal rights for women and slaves.

The division set up by the new atheists between superior Western, rational values and the irrational beliefs of those outside our tradition is not only unhistorical but untrue. The East and the West do not have separate, competing value systems. We do not treat life with greater sanctity than those we belittle and dismiss. Eastern and Western traditions have within them varied ethical systems, some of which are repugnant and some of which are worth emulating. To hold up the highest ideals of our own culture and to deny that these great ideals exist in other cultures, especially Eastern cultures, is made possible only by a staggering historical and cultural illiteracy. The civilization we champion and promote as superior is, in fact, a product of the fusion of traditions and beliefs of the Orient and the Occident. We advance morally and intellectually only when we cross these cultural lines, when we use the lens of other cultures to examine our own. It is then that we see our limitations, that we uncover the folly of our own assumptions and our prejudices. It is then that we achieve empathy, we learn and make wisdom possible.

Muslim societies are colored far more by national characteristics. An Islamic Iraqi is likely to have a culture and outlook on life quite different from that of an Islamic
Indonesian, just as a French Catholic is likely to have an outlook different from that of a Bolivian Catholic. Nearly all
Muslim suicide bombers come from the Arabic-speaking
countries. Most Muslims, like most Arabs, want nothing to
do with these people. I have stood over the bodies—including the bodies of children—left in the wake of suicide bombings by Islamic militants in Jerusalem. I have also knelt
beside the frail, thin bodies of boys shot for sport by Israeli
soldiers in the Gaza strip. What is the moral difference? I do
not see one.

Terrorists arise in all cultures, all nations and all religions. Terrorists lurk within our own society. The bombing
on April 19, 1995, of the Alfred P. Murrah Federal Building in
Oklahoma City killed 168 people—19 of them children—and
injured hundreds. It was carried out by an American citizen
named Timothy McVeigh. William Krar and Judith Bruey of
Noonday, Texas, pleaded guilty in 2003 to possession of a
weapon of mass destruction. Investigators found inside their
home and in three storage facilities a sodium cyanide bomb
capable of killing thousands, more than a hundred explosives, half a million rounds of ammunition, dozens of illegal
weapons, and a mound of white-supremacist and antigovern-
ment literature. McVeigh was not a Muslim; neither was
Krar or Bruey. None of these people was inspired to acts of

terror by religion. Terrorists, for all their claims of religious martyrdom and noble self-sacrifice, are criminals. They mask their indiscriminate violence with noble abstractions, but they are all morally depraved.

Joseph Conrad's *The Secret Agent* and *Heart of Darkness*, along with Fyodor Dostoevsky's *The Demons* and *Crime and Punishment*, give some of the best insights into the well-springs of terror. Conrad and Dostoevsky saw the breakup of personal identity, alienation, feelings of collective and personal humiliation and shame as the forces that fed acts of horrific violence. Revolutionary political change, whether dressed up in the language of religion, anarchy, fascism or communism, was another form of criminality. Revolutionary elites are as infected with the lust for violence and penchant for hypocrisy as the political and social order they seek to overthrow.

In Dostoevsky's *Crime and Punishment*, Raskolnikov, imprisoned in Siberia for the murder of a pawnbroker and her sister, has a nightmare in the prison hospital that the world "was doomed to fall victim to some terrible, as yet unknown and unseen pestilence."[9] This plague convinces people that they alone know the truth. The plague unleashes collective insanity, yet "never, never had people considered themselves so intelligent and unshakable in the truth as did these infected ones. Never had they thought their judgment, their scientific conclusions, their moral convictions and beliefs more unshakable."[10] Those infected with the plague "each thought the truth was contained in himself alone, and suffered looking at others, beat his breast, wept, and wrung his hands." [11] This plague soon engulfed Russia. The insidious pestilence Raskolnikov feared has infected these atheists, as well as religious fundamentalists.

The promotion of violence as a cleansing or purifying agent is not limited, however, to revolutionaries and terrorists. It beats in the heart of the advanced, industrialized states, which also accept that some people must be murdered to eradicate human contamination.

Conrad's novel *Heart of Darkness* exposed the corrupt heart of civilized Europe. The great institutions of European imperial powers and noble ideals of European enlightenment, as Conrad saw in the Congo, were covers for rapacious greed, exploitation and barbarity. Kurtz is the self-deluded megalomaniac ivory trader in *Heart of Darkness* who plants the shriveled heads of murdered Congolese on pikes outside his remote trading station. But Kurtz is also highly educated and refined. Conrad describes him as an orator, writer, poet, musician and the respected chief agent of the ivory company's Inner Station. He is "an emissary of pity, and science, and progress." [12] Kurtz was "a universal genius" [13] and "a very remarkable person." [14] He is a prodigy, at once gifted and multitalented. He comes to Africa fired by noble ideals and virtues. He ends his life as a murderous tyrant who thought he was a god.

"His mother was half-English, his father was half-

French," Conrad wrote of Kurtz. "All Europe contributed to the making of Kurtz; and by-the-by I learned that, most appropriately, the International Society for the Suppression of Savage Customs had entrusted him with the making of a report, for its future guidance. . . . He began with the argument that we whites, from the point of development we had arrived at, 'must necessarily appear to them [savages] in the nature of supernatural beings—we approach them with the might as of a deity,' and so on, and so on. 'By the simple exercise of our will we can exert a power for good practically unbounded,' etc., etc. From that point he soared and took me with him. The peroration was magnificent, though difficult to remember, you know. It gave me the notion of an exotic Immensity ruled by an august Benevolence. It made me tingle with enthusiasm. This was the unbounded power of eloquence—of words—of burning noble words. There were no practical hints to interrupt the magic current of phrases, unless a kind of note at the foot of the last page, scrawled evidently much later, in an unsteady hand, may be regarded as the exposition of a method. It was very simple, and at the end of that moving appeal to every altruistic sentiment it blazed at you, luminous and terrifying, like a flash of lightning in a serene sky: 'Exterminate all the brutes!' " [15]

As Conrad knew, the vision of an enlightened West that spread civilization to a savage world is not supported by history. The worst genocides and slaughters of the last century were perpetrated by highly advanced industrialized nations. Muslims, including Saddam Hussein's brutal regime, have a long way to go before they reach the body count of the Nazis or the Soviet Union or the Chinese communists. It was, in fact, the Muslim-led government in Bosnia that practiced tolerance while Serbian Orthodox Christians carried out most of the ethnic cleansing in a war that left 250,000 dead. Some 10,000 ethnic Serbs remained in Sarajevo and fought alongside the Bosnia Muslims. The city's Jewish community, dating back to 1492, also stayed behind. The worst atrocities in Bosnia were sanctified not by imams, but by Catholic and Serbian Orthodox priests.

Terror is delivered in many forms. The industrial nations are not immune from employing terror. The only country that has deployed the greatest weapon of mass terror—the atomic bomb—is the United States. General Dwight Eisenhower opposed using the atomic bomb on a civilian population. He was overruled. The bomb was dropped for its psychological and emotional impact. It was meant to shock and demoralize not only the Japanese population, who were already on the verge of surrender, but also the Soviets, who, political leaders in Washington hoped, would be intimidated by the devastating effects of the blast.

"That fateful summer. Eight–fifteen," said Hiroshima's mayor, Tadatoshi Akiba, on the August 6, 2007, anniversary of the bombing. "The roar of a B-29 breaks the morning calm. A parachute opens in the blue sky. Then suddenly, a flash, an enormous blast—silence—hell on Earth. The eyes of young girls watching the parachute were melted. Their faces became giant charred blisters. The skin of people seeking help dangled from their fingernails. Their hair stood on end. Their clothes were ripped to shreds. People trapped in houses toppled by the blast were burned alive. Others died when their eyeballs and internal organs burst from their bodies—Hiroshima was a hell where those who somehow survived envied the dead.

"Within the year," he said, "140,000 had died. Many who escaped death initially are still suffering from leukemia, thyroid cancer, and a vast array of other afflictions. But there was more. Sneered at for their keloid scars, discriminated against in employment and marriage, unable to find understanding for profound emotional wounds, survivors suffered and struggled day after day, questioning the meaning of life." [16]

The murder of innocent civilians was defended as a legitimate way to respond to the collective humiliation suffered by the United States during the Japanese attack on Pearl Harbor. "The Japanese began the war from the air at Pearl Harbor," said President Truman in his first official statement after the bombing. "They have been repaid manyfold." The annihilation of 140,000 people at Hiroshima and 70,000 at Nagasaki (overwhelmingly civilians), the deaths of thousands of others from radiation sickness, and the obliteration of two cities was considered appropriate retaliation for an air raid on a military target that killed fewer than 2,500.

The American military planners picked Hiroshima because the bombers would face less anti-aircraft fire. They calculated that the effect of obliterating a huge civilian population would be dramatic and terrifying. The "Strategic Bombing Survey," conducted at President Harry Truman's request after the bomb hit Hiroshima on August 6, 1945, noted that "nearly all the school children . . . were at work in the open," to be exploded, irradiated or incinerated in the perfect firestorm. Thousands of children on their way to school in Hiroshima and Nagasaki died. It had, as the planners at the University of California–run Los Alamos Lab envisioned, the maximum psychological impact.

The 370,000 overall deaths attributed to the bombings, 85 percent of which were civilian, do not permit us to place ourselves on a higher moral plane than terrorists. The use of an atomic weapon on noncombatants is not "regrettable but necessary." It is not part of the cost of war. It is morally indefensible. But heading into this kind of introspection is disturbing. It raises questions that shatter our self-image and question our moral purity. It is this realization of our own innate capacity for barbarity that sees Kurtz sputter at the end of his life: "The horror, the horror!"

Conrad grasped the irredeemable corruption of humanity. The "civilized" virtues that drove Kurtz into the jungle veiled abject self-interest, unchecked greed and murder. Conrad was in the Congo in the late nineteenth century when the Belgian monarch King Leopold was plundering the country. The Belgian occupation resulted in the death, by disease, starvation and murder, of some 10 million Congolese. Conrad understood what we did to others in the name of civilization and progress. This theme is also central to Conrad's earlier work "An Outpost of Progress." He writes of two white traders, Carlier and Kayerts, who are sent to a remote trading station in the Congo. The mission is endowed with a great moral purpose: to export European "civilization" to Africa. But the boredom and lack of social constraints swiftly turns the two men into savages. They trade slaves for ivory. They get into a feud over dwindling food supplies, and Kayerts shoots and kills his unarmed companion Carlier:

> They were two perfectly insignificant and incapable individuals whose existence is only rendered possible through high organization of civilized crowds. Few men realize that their life, the very essence of their character, their capabilities and their audacities, are only the expression of their belief in the safety of their surroundings. The courage, the composure, the confidence; the emotions and principles; every great and every insignificant thought belongs not to the individual but to the crowd; to the crowd that believes blindly in the irresistible force of its institutions and its morals, in the power of its police and of

its opinion. But the contact with pure unmitigated savagery, with primitive nature and primitive man, brings sudden and profound trouble into the heart. To the sentiment of being alone of one's kind, to the clear perception of the loneliness of one's thoughts, of one's sensations—to the negation of the habitual, which is safe, there is added the affirmation of the unusual, which is dangerous; a suggestion of things vague, uncontrollable, and repulsive, whose discomposing intrusion excites the imagination and tries the civilized nerves of the foolish and the wise alike.[17]

The Managing Director of the Great Civilizing Company—for, as Conrad notes, "civilization" follows trade—arrives by steamer at the end of the story. He is not met at the dock by his two agents. He climbs the steep bank to the trading station with the captain and engine-driver behind him. The director finds Kayerts, who, after the murder, committed suicide by hanging himself by a leather strap from a cross that marked the grave of the previous station chief. Kayerts' toes are a couple of inches above the ground. His arms hang stiffly down, "and, irreverently, he was putting out a swollen tongue at his Managing Director."[18]

Conrad saw cruelty as part of human nature. This cruelty arrives, however, in different forms. Stable, industrialized societies, awash in wealth and privilege, can better construct systems that mask this cruelty, although it is nakedly displayed in their imperial outposts. In these zones of safety, we are lulled into the illusion that human beings can become rational and "civilized." The war on terror is another in a series of campaigns by those who practice barbarity and violence in the name of idealism and utopia. Evil, for these idealists, lies beyond us. It contaminates our enemies, but not ourselves. Once we root out this evil we will all progress and advance together.

"To see that our problem is with Islam itself, and not merely with 'terrorism,' we need only ask ourselves *why* Muslim terrorists do what they do," writes Harris. "The answer is that men like bin Laden *actually* believe what they say they believe. They believe in the literal truth of the Koran. Why did nineteen well-educated, middle-class men trade their lives in this world for the privilege of killing thousands of our neighbors? Because they believed that they would go straight to paradise for doing so. It is rare to find the behavior of human beings so fully and satisfactorily explained. Why have we been reluctant to accept this explanation?"[19]

Those who externalize evil and seek to eradicate this evil lose touch with their own humanity and the humanity of others. They can no longer make moral distinctions. They are blind to their own moral corruption. In the name of civilization and great virtues, in the name of reason and science, they urge us to become monsters. It is this inverted logic that allows these atheists to sign on for the worst curtailment of our liberties, the broad abasement of basic human rights, permanent war and the use of torture.

"Given what many of us believe about the exigencies of our war on terrorism, the practice of torture, in certain circumstances, would seem to be not only permissible, but necessary," Harris writes.[20]

"What is the difference between pursuing a course of action where we run the risk of inadvertently subjecting some innocent men to torture, and pursuing one in which we will inadvertently kill far greater numbers of men, women, and children?" he asks. "Rather, it seems obvious that the misapplication of torture should be far less troubling to us than collateral damage: there are, after all, no infants interned at Guantánamo Bay, just rather scrofulous young men, many of whom were caught in the very act of trying to kill our soldiers. Torture need not even impose a significant risk of death or permanent injury, while the collaterally damaged are, almost by definition, crippled or killed. The ethical divide that seems to be opening up here suggests that those who are willing to drop bombs might want to abduct the nearest and dearest of suspected terrorists—their wives, mothers, and daughters—and torture them as well, assuming anything profitable to our side might come of it."[21]

Those who waterboard detainees, strip them of all legal rights and let them rot in physical and moral black holes defend their actions as a "necessity." Harris quotes the Harvard law professor Alan Dershowitz, who defends torture by offering the ticking time bomb scenario. Dershowitz says that if a terrorist has planted a bomb in the center of a city we should be allowed to torture him to find the bomb and prevent catastrophe. Harris adds that we must dust off "a strappado" and expose "this unpleasant fellow to a suasion of bygone times."[22] A strappado suspends a victim in the air by means of a rope attached to his hands, which are tied behind his back. It is optional to add weights to the body. It is a torture technique inherited from the Inquisition. It is also known as "reverse hanging" or "Palestinian hanging," because of its use by Israeli security forces. It was used by the Nazis at Auschwitz. Manadel al-Jamadi was killed in November 2003 by U.S. forces when he was strappadoed during an "interrogation session" at Abu Ghraib prison in Iraq. The U.S. military ruled his death a homicide.

Human evil is not a problem. It is a mystery. It cannot be solved. It is a bitter, constant paradox that is part of human nature. When one evil appears vanquished a new one rises to take its place. The forces of darkness are our own forces. If we fail to name or acknowledge these forces, they will destroy us. Acknowledgment means accepting that our encounter with evil is permanent and perpetual. We must always anticipate it. We must work against it. We must be vigilant to conscience. The belief that we can achieve human perfection, that we can advance morally, is itself an evil. It provides a cover for criminality and abuse, a justification for murder. It sanctifies war, murder and torture for an unattainable absolute. It denies our own moral pollution. It reduces human beings to the status of a virus. And it turns us into brutes. Those who permit torture and war in their own names empower sadists and psychopaths. They consign whole populations to moral and physical oblivion. They become, as Conrad and Dostoevsky knew, as morally depraved as those they oppose. They sink to barbarity, all the while exalting themselves as saviors. They become Kurtz. They become insane. They forget what it is to be human.

CHAPTER SEVEN

The Illusive Self

> Dressed in a little brief authority,
> Most ignorant of what he's most assured,
> His glassy essence, like an angry ape
> Plays such fantastic tricks before high heaven
> As makes the angels weep.
> —William Shakespeare,
> *Measure for Measure*, 1.2. 144–148[1]

Our collective and personal histories—the stories we tell about ourselves to ourselves and others—are used to avoid facing the incoherence and fragmentation of our lives. Chaos, chance and irrational urges, often locked in our unconscious, propel, inform and direct us. Our self is elusive. It is not fixed. It is subject to forces often beyond our control. To be human is to be captive to these forces, forces we cannot always name or understand. We mutate and change. We are not who we were. We are not who we will become. The familiarity of habit and ritual, as well as the narratives we invent to give structure and meaning to our life, helps hide this fragmentation. But human life is fluid and inconsistent. Those who place their faith in a purely rational existence begin from the premise that human beings can have fixed and determined selves governed by reason and knowledge. This is itself an act of faith.

We can veto a response or check an impulse, reason can direct our actions, but we are just as often hostage to the pulls of the instinctual, the irrational and the unconscious. We can rationalize our actions later, but this does not make them rational. The social and individual virtues we promote as universal values that must be attained by the rest of the human species are more often narrow, socially conditioned responses hardwired into us for our collective and personal survival and advancement. These values are rarely disinterested. They nearly always justify our right to dominance and power.

We do not digest every sensation and piece of information we encounter. To do so would leave us paralyzed. The bandwidth of consciousness—our ability to transmit information measured in bits per second—is too narrow to register the enormous mass of external information we receive and act upon. We are assaulted with about 14 million bits of information per second. The bandwidth of consciousness is around 18 bits per second. We have conscious access to about a millionth of the information we use to function in life. Much of the information we receive and our subsequent responses do not take place on the level of consciousness. As the philosopher John Gray points out, irrational and subconscious forces, however unacknowledged, are as potent within us as in others.[2]

"It is assumed that the identity of the person rests on that of consciousness," the philosopher Arthur Schopenhauer wrote:

> If, however, we understand by this merely the conscious recollection of the course of life, then it is not enough. We know, it is true, something more of the course of our life than of a novel we have formerly read, yet very little indeed. The principal events, the interesting scenes, have been impressed on us; for the rest, a thousand events are forgotten for one that has been retained. The older we become, the more does everything pass us by without a trace . . . . It is true that, in consequence of our relation to the external world, we are accustomed to regard the subject of knowing, the knowing I, as our real self . . . . This, however, is the mere function of the brain, and is not our real self. Our true self, the kernel of our inner nature, is that which is to be found behind this, and which really knows nothing but willing and non-willing . . . [3]

To accept the intractable and irrational forces that drive us, to admit that these forces are as entrenched in us as in all human beings, is to relinquish the fantasy that the human species can have total, rational control over human destiny. It is to accept our limitations, to live within the confines of human nature. Ethical, moral, religious and political systems that do not concede these stark limitations have nothing to say to us. The new atheists, like all utopians, ask us to live unexamined lives, to believe we can conquer our humanness.

Knowledge is not wisdom. Knowledge is the domain of scientific and intellectual inquiry. Wisdom goes beyond self-awareness. It permits us to interpret the rational and the nonrational. It is both intellectual and intuitive. And those who remain trapped within the confines of knowledge and pedantry do not commune with the larger world. They cannot see or speak to the deeper truths of life. This is why we turn, especially in our moments of deepest despair or greatest joy, to artistic and religious expression. The expression of the sacred, part of the human desire to preserve and honor that which cannot be tallied and quantified, is what makes the ritual and the liturgy of religious life powerful and real, despite the corruption of the institutions behind them.

Literature and the arts often realize human truths well before other branches of human endeavor. For centuries, poets, novelists and dramatists have spoken of the instability of the self and the power of ritual before the transcendent. Art itself is one such ritual. Art, like religion, looks beyond historical truths. It explores particular "singular" events, to uncover, as Aristotle wrote in his Poetics, "philosophical" truths of what "probably or necessarily" happens. These universal or philosophical truths, Aristotle pointed out, are manifested in poetry and art rather than history, and without art we do not see them.[4]

In her novel *The Song of the Lark*, Willa Cather writes that the Native Americans of the Southwest made pottery to house water once they had housed themselves. All their customs and ceremonies and their religion went back to water, which was one of the essential elements of life. The pottery was "their most direct appeal to water, the envelope and sheath of the precious element itself." She continues:

> When Thea took her bath at the bottom of the canyon, in the sunny pool behind the screen of cottonwoods, she sometimes felt as if the water must have sovereign qualities, from having been the object of so much service and desire. That stream was the only living thing left of the drama that had been played out in the canyon centuries ago. In the rapid, restless heart of it, flowing swifter than the rest, there was a continuity of life that reached back into the old time. The glittering thread of current had a kind of lightly worn, loosely knit personality, graceful and laughing. Thea's bath came to have a ceremonial gravity. The atmosphere of the canyon was ritualistic.

One morning, as she was standing upright in the pool, splashing water between her shoulder-blades with a big sponge, something flashed through her mind that made her draw herself up and stand still until the water had quite dried upon her flushed skin. The stream and the broken pottery: what was any art but an effort to make a sheath, a mould in which to imprison for a moment the shining, elusive element which is life itself—life hurrying past us and running away, too strong to stop, too sweet to lose? The Indian women had held it in their jars. In the sculpture she had seen in the Art Institute, it had been caught in a flash of arrested motion. In singing, one made a vessel of one's throat and nostrils and held it on one's breath, caught the stream in a scale of natural intervals.[5]

All human actions that confront the mysterious forces that make life possible involve acts of ritual and improvisation. Communication, as Tzvetan Todorov writes, is "both paradigm and syntagm, code and context; man has just as much need to communicate with the world as with men."[6] Those who focus only on human communication, who are unable to step outside the realm of prosaic knowledge, sever themselves from the sacred. They remain trapped in a deadening self-awareness. They lose the capacity to honor and protect that which makes life possible.

"Self-awareness is as much a disability as a power," the philosopher John Gray writes. "The most accomplished pianist is not the one who is most aware of her movements when she plays. The best craftsman may not know how he works. Very often we are at our most skillful when we are least self-aware. That may be why many cultures have sought to disrupt or diminish self-conscious awareness. In Japan, archers are taught that they will hit the target only when they no longer think of it—or themselves."[7]

Artists, who draw upon the mercurial undercurrents of the subconscious, face a truth about human consciousness. They are informed by the intuitive, unarticulated meanderings of the human psyche. This wisdom, which often lies beyond precise expression, transcends what is constructed by the plodding conscious mind. Actor Uta Hagen in her book *Respect for Acting* discusses the rift between voluntary and involuntary memory for those attempting to resurrect authentic emotions on stage:

> To bring about tears, the beginning actor's tendency is to think sad things, to pump for that mood or that general state of being, to try to remember a sad occasion, the story of that occasion, and then pray to God that somehow he will be catapulted into an appropriate emotional response somewhere along the way. I used to make all of these mistakes and . . . sometimes I managed to work myself into a near trauma offstage, which brought me on [stage] with the sensation of moving in glue. After a few years, I discovered intuitively that what sent me correctly

[into an authentic emotional reaction] was a tiny remembered object only indirectly connected with the sad event: a polka-dot tie, an ivy leaf on a stucco wall, a smell or sound of sizzling bacon, a grease spot on the upholstery, things as seemingly illogical as those . . . [8]

Hagen later learned from the psychiatrist Jacques Palaci that because these trigger objects were only perceived peripherally at the moment of crisis, they had escaped the mind's "reasoning censor,"[9] the coping mechanism that attempts to block any loss of control. And because these tiny irrational objects had evaded the censor, they still retained within them the power to unlock and revive long-distant pain, a power denied to the rational mind.

Marcel Proust explored the tricks and illusions of memory. *In Search of Lost Time* repeatedly probed memory, how it worked and how it empowered and shaped human perception. Voluntary memory—the willed, conscious retention of our past—held little value for him. This form of remembering, he understood, is always partial. The images it chooses are arbitrary and remote from reality. The conscious memories we retain are like the pages of a photo album. They fail to capture the essence of the past, to momentarily erase time, to bring us back to the world we once inhabited. Our deepest remembered sensations are not a product of willed consciousness, of voluntary memory. These sensations are only possible through involuntary memory, over which we have no control. Involuntary memory is explosive, sudden and unpredictable. It instantly, and without warning, momentarily restores the past. This visceral and total experience of involuntary memory comes upon us in a flash of recognition. It lifts us out of time and space. Voluntary memory, the efforts we consciously make to remember, captures little more than Plato's shadows on the cave wall. Volcanic emotions are buried like land mines within us, waiting to be detonated by a smell, a landscape, a word or the repetition of a moment or ritual lost to our rational self. These hidden realms of visceral, irrational emotions drive us as powerfully, perhaps more powerfully, than the rational constructs we build around them. They shatter our meticulously constructed self, plunging us into the chaos of existence.

"It is a labor in vain to attempt to recapture it: all efforts of our intellect must prove futile," Proust wrote of our conscious effort to evoke our past. "The past is hidden somewhere outside the realm, beyond the intellect, in some material object (in the sensation which that material object will give us) of which we have no inkling. And it depends on chance whether or not we come upon this object before we ourselves must die." [10]:

> For with the perturbations of memory are linked the intermittencies of the heart. It is, no doubt, the existence of our body, which we may compare to a vase enclosing our spir-

itual nature, that induces us to suppose that all our inner wealth, our past joys, all our sorrows, are perpetually in our possession. Perhaps it is equally inexact to suppose that they escape or return. In any case if they remain within us, for most of the time it is in an unknown region where they are of no use to us, and where even the most ordinary are crowded out by memories of a different level, which precludes any simultaneous occurrence of them in our consciousness. But if the context of sensations in which they are preserved is recaptured, they acquire in turn the same power of expelling everything that is incompatible with them, of installing alone in us the self that originally lived them.[11]

The narrator in *In Search of Lost Time*, "after a dreary day with the prospect of a depressing morrow,"[12] raises to his lips a spoonful of the tea in which he had soaked a morsel of a small cake known as a petite madeleine. When he tastes the mixture of tea and cake, a shudder runs through him. "An exquisite pleasure had invaded my senses, something isolated, detached, with no suggestion of its origin," Proust writes. "And at once the vicissitudes of life had become indifferent to me, its disasters innocuous, its brevity illusory—this new sensation having had on me the effect which love has of filling me with a precious essence; or rather this essence was not in me, it *was* me. I had ceased now to feel mediocre, contingent, mortal."[13]

These transcendent moments are unsettling, for they shatter our constructed realities and narratives of ourselves. The mind has overtaken itself; we feel "an abyss of uncertainty."[14] We face, as we do in dreams, powerful forces over which we have no control. We see, if only for a moment, that the personalities we have constructed to define ourselves are a series of plagiarisms.

The memory evoked by these experiences bypasses the leaden plodding of the intellect. The taste of the madeleine instantly brings the narrator back to the Sunday mornings at Combray. He is again a boy about to say good morning to his Aunt Léonie in the old gray house before going to mass. She would give him a madeleine, dipping it first in her own cup of tea or tisane. The sight of the madeleine had recalled nothing before he tasted it. The images of madeleines had slowly dissociated themselves from his childhood.

"But when from a long-distant past nothing subsists," Proust wrote, "after the people are dead, after the things are broken and scattered, taste and smell alone, more fragile but more enduring, more unsubstantial, more persistent, more faithful, remain poised a long time, like souls, remembering, waiting, hoping, amid the ruins of all the rest; and bear unflinchingly, in the tiny and almost impalpable drop of their essence, the vast structure of recollection."[15]

These involuntary memories are impervious to rational control. They arrive and vanish without premeditation. Memory, when shaped and manipulated by the intellect alone, imprisons us. When memory arrives unawares and thrusts us outside of time, it frees us. It is the power of involuntary memory that reminds us of the feebleness and incompleteness of the rational self and conscious thought. It exposes the fragmented nature of the self, a fragmentation that renders our past selves as strangers to us. It mocks the delusion that life can be rational, ordered and coherent.

Proust's narrator, toward the end of the novel, finds that as time passes he is no longer able to grieve for his dead lover. He realizes that the self is not constant, that there is a new self within him that "would find it easy to endure the prospect of life without Albertine."[16] This change horrifies him. He sees that his grief will be replaced with indifference.

"The possible advent of these new selves, which ought each to bear a different name for the preceding one, was something I had always dreaded, because of their indifference to the object of my love," Proust writes.[17]

The old self, the self that was prostrated by grief, had become a shell. The old self had vanished. The self that ardently felt love, affection and terrible loss had died with Albertine. We decay, die and renew. But it takes a great grief and its gradual abatement to see how we change with time, and, as Proust wrote, we "become another person to whom sufferings of his predecessor are no more than the sufferings of a stranger, of which we can speak with compassion because we do not feel them. Indeed, we are unconcerned about having undergone all those sufferings, since we have only a vague remembrance of having suffered them." [18]

> This new self had some contact with the old: as a friend who is indifferent to a bereavement speaks of it nevertheless to the persons present in a suitable tone of sorrow, and returns from time to time to the room in which the widower who has asked him to receive the company for him may still be heard weeping. I too still wept when I became once again for a moment the former friend of Albertine. But it was into a new personality that I was tending to change altogether. It is not because other people are dead that our affection for them fades; it is because we ourselves are dying. [19]

We are not, as Proust understood, unitary human beings with established identities and constant selves. We, as distinct individuals and as a species, have no fixed coherence. The more we attempt to build monuments to ourselves, the more we live behind the walls of self-constructed prisons. This is the central message of the Book of Ecclesiastes. The author, known as Koheleth, was a realist. He sees the pathetic, vain project we spend a lifetime constructing, the "unhappy business that God has given to human beings to be busy with." He cautions his readers to look at "all the deeds that are done under the sun; and see, all is vanity and a chasing after wind." The word he uses for vanity is *hebel,* which is also used for mist or vapor. It is emptiness, the root meaning of the Vulgate's *vanitas.* It is conceptually like the word *shunyata* or "void" in Buddhist thought. Koheleth knew "that nothing is certain or permanent, real or unreal," that "all things are wearisome." The "eye is not satisfied with seeing, or the ear filled with hearing. What has been is what will be, and what has been done is what will be done." He tells us that "what is crooked cannot be made straight, and what is lacking cannot be counted," and he knows that God has "put a sense of past and future into their minds, yet they cannot find out what God has done from the beginning to the end." All our goals and aims, all the little human schemes we embark upon in life, carry within them the potential for bitter self-destruction.

In Ecclesiastes it is not what we do in life, but what we do with what life gives us. We have few real choices. We carry our human flaws to the grave. Our attempts to become god-like, to deny the emptiness, rhythms and cycles of life, are vanity. The best we can do is endure with compassion, wisdom and humility, and accept the ambiguity and ultimate mystery of existence.

Detachment without withdrawal, Ecclesiastes writes, is one of the secrets of wisdom. Death awaits us all. We must give up on the notion that one is rewarded for virtue, that we can save ourselves from our human predicament or that we can morally advance as a species. We remain trapped by human nature. We must battle with it, as Koheleth battled with it centuries before us. The evil and the good endure the same hardships and blessings. But Ecclesiastes reminds us that God has put *'olam* into man's mind. *'Olam* means "eternity." It denotes mystery or obscurity. We do not know what this mystery, this eternity, means. This eternity teases us, as Keats wrote, out of thought. And once we recognize it and face it, simplistic answers no longer work. Our vain belief in our own powers, in our reason and perfectibility, is exposed as a fraud. As Northrop Frye rightly points out, Ecclesiastes sees the emptiness around us, the emptiness of those who trust in their own power and live in self-delusion.[20] And in Ecclesiastes, which often troubles biblical literalists and those who believe we are moving toward a glorious finale, we find the best of ancient wisdom.

Those who turn to religion seek an expression of the transcendent and the sacred. Few believers care much for dogma. Many religious institutions, such as the Catholic Church, incorporate ideologically diverse movements, from Opus Dei to liberation theology. All Catholics, however, are unified in the liturgy and ritual of the sacraments. The pope can rail against birth control and publish turgid encyclicals, but for most Catholics his theological admonishments go unheeded.

The passages of most sacred texts in all religions are of little real importance. Believers pick and choose what fits. They discard the rest. The liberal Presbyterian Church, in which I grew up, ignored the violent, apocalyptic literature in

Daniel and Revelation, as well as the homophobic and misogynist rants by Paul. They were expunged—along with the calls by God to the Israelites to carry out acts of righteous genocide—from the biblical readings at the lectern. These passages might as well have been cut out of our Bibles. Christian fundamentalists, who seek a justification for their bigotry and hatred, trumpet these passages and rarely speak of the Sermon on the Mount, Christ's calls for vows of poverty and His pacifism.

Such selective interpretation is no different for Muslims, Jews, Hindus, Buddhists and other believers. It is culture, history, circumstance, tradition, economics and the deep self-interest of the tribe or the nation that more powerfully inform belief systems than the contradictory and often impenetrable pages of the Bible, the Koran or any other sacred text. Attempts by these atheists to reduce sacred texts to instruction manuals is not part of the reality of belief. Faith arises out of practice. We find our faith in how we live. The labels we attach to ourselves—Christian, Buddhist, Jew, Muslim or atheist—are a way to tell stories about ourselves, to create coherent narratives.

The danger we face does not come from religion. It comes from a growing intellectual bankruptcy that is one of the symptoms of a dying culture. In ancient Rome, as the republic disintegrated and the Caesars were deified, as the Roman Senate became little more than an echo chamber of the emperor, the population's attention was diverted by a series of frontier wars and violent and elaborate spectacles in the arena. The excitement of entertainment consumed ancient Rome's emotional and intellectual life. It poisoned civic and political discourse. Social critics no longer had a forum in which to speak. They were answered with ridicule and rage. It was not the prerogative of the citizen to think.

We have been robbed of the physical spaces where we could once carry out meaningful discourse and debate, where we could participate in our society as citizens. Community centers, village squares and town meetings, the public spaces that made democratic participation possible, have been replaced by privatized space, by shopping malls, where we are permitted to enter as consumers and forbidden to enter as citizens. The privatization of public space has pushed us into the lonely virtual worlds of television and the Internet. It has cut us off from others. These isolated, deadening virtual worlds are curious hybrids. They give us the illusion of being part of a powerful (although anonymous) community. Sentimental drama and tawdry spectacle, from "reality" television shows to huge sporting events and saccharine musicals, fill the empty caverns of our inner life. These spectacles have become the common cultural experience and provide the common vocabulary for communication. We sit for hours alone in front of screens. We are enraptured and diverted by bread and circuses. And while we sit mesmerized, corporations steadily dismantle the democratic state. We are kept ignorant and entertained.

Our return to an image-based culture means the destruction of the abstract thought made possible by a literate, print-based society. Image-based societies do not grasp or cope with ambiguity, nuance, doubt and the many layers of irrational motives and urges, some of them frightening, that make human actions complex and finally unfathomable. They eschew self-criticism for amusement. They build fantastic non-reality-based belief systems that cater to human desires and illusions rather than human reality. These illusions, whether religious or secular, offer a simple and unexamined myth that the human race is advancing morally, spiritually and materially toward paradise. This advance is proclaimed as inevitable. This faith in our advancement makes us passive and complacent.

Believers in the Bible, as well as the Koran, were asked to embrace a hidden deity. The second of the Ten Commandments prohibits the Israelites from making images of the Lord. This new deity could not be captured in pictures, statues or any concrete, iconographic form. God existed in the word and through the word, a radical concept in the ancient world. To worship God without physical representations of God made it appear as if believers were worshipping nothing. It was to give up security. It was to believe in a God that could not be seen or controlled. It was to live with paradox, uncertainty and doubt. It was to accept anxiety. To believe in this deity required abstract thinking. It made possible the moral life.

God answered Moses' request for revelation with these words: "I AM WHO I AM." This phrase is probably more accurately translated "I WILL BE WHAT I WILL BE." God was an experience. God came in the profound flashes of insight that cut through the darkness, in the hope that permitted human beings to cope with inevitable despair and suffering. God came in the healing solidarity of love and self-sacrifice.

Paul Tillich catches these truths when he writes, "The courage to be is rooted in the God who appears when God has disappeared in the anxiety of doubt."[21]

All this is being lost. The modern world, with its vast, soulless urban enclaves, is divorcing itself from the rhythms of nature and community. Our days are filled with mindless tasks, the drudgery of work and a gnawing loneliness. The mental pollution of sound bites, the dizzying and ceaseless chatter of television and computers, the constant assault of advertising seek to fill the void with a virtual, image-based illusion. This world is escapist. We are bombarded, thousands of times a day, with the emotional simplicity and terrible beauty of lies. And we believe them. We believe them because they make us feel, at least for a moment, better and empowered. We increasingly lack the intellectual and self-critical tools to disentangle this net of lies from truth.

"Our present-day civilization is full of mass delusions, prejudices, and collective errors which can be recognized easily if viewed from above, but which cannot be detected if they are seen from within," wrote Joost A. M. Meerloo. "While the delusion of witchcraft has been banished, we have never freed ourselves from the delusion of cultural or racial inferiority and superiority. Medieval mass obsessions such as tarantism and Saint Vitus' dance are little known now among Western nations; in their place we have mass meetings with shouting and crowds expressing in a delusional ecstasy their affiliation to some political delusion. Instead of the dance fury, we have the raving frenzy of the motor, or the passive peeping contagion of the television screen." [22]

Those who control our political and social discourse, our news and educational systems have become adept at manipulating images. These images evoke emotional responses rather than convey factual information. We confuse emotions with knowledge, and we confuse knowledge with wisdom. "Our politics, religion, news, athletics, education and commerce have been transformed into congenial adjuncts of show business, largely without protest or even much popular notice," wrote Neil Postman. "The result is that we are a people on the verge of amusing ourselves to death." [23]

The new atheists are products of the morally stunted world of entertainment. Despite their insistence that they have cornered the market on rationality, they appeal to neither our reason nor our intellect. They appeal to our deepest and most irrational subliminal desires. They feed our illusions. They manipulate our yearnings with the same skill as the corporate advertisers, the political spin doctors, the entertainment industry, the Bible-thumping televangelists who promise miracles, and the cable news networks who speak to us in the language of nationalistic cant. Public discourse is about how we feel, or how we are made to feel. The simple slogans these atheists repeat about religion do not communicate ideas. They amuse us. They bolster our self-satisfaction, anti-intellectualism and provincialism.

Edward Bernays, who was Sigmund Freud's nephew, turned in the 1920s to Freud and psychoanalysis to create the modern public relations profession. He understood that people could be sold things they did not need by linking mass-produced goods to unconscious desires. He eroticized the car. He pioneered celebrity endorsements. He persuaded women to take up smoking as a sign of independence. Cigarettes, at the time of his campaign, were called "freedom torches." Bernays began the psychological techniques of modern propaganda to create a docile and easily manipulated population. Government agencies, corporations and the CIA soon adopted these tactics to mold and direct public perceptions. Many who live in the United States, plagued by its consumer culture, waste their energy attempting to satisfy the insatiable demands of an all-consuming self. People have become cut off, engulfed in the fruitless search to find an unachievable happiness in the things they accumulate, the experiences and products they are sold, or the careers they have built. The promised self-fulfillment, of course, never arrives. Consumers are prodded with even greater urgency to seek solace in newer products, greater opulence and increased status. The frantic search for happiness is endless, "since," as Proust wrote, "what one has obtained is never anything but a new starting-point for further desires." [24]

The techniques of control in an image-based, anticommunal, consumerist culture are used for governing. The focus group was invented by psychoanalysts to shape our desires and passions. American democracy has become a consumer fraud. Those who practice these techniques are manipulative and cynical. They have robbed us of art, of democratic rights, of education, of respect for the world around us, of the sacred, and they have left us sputtering to each other in the simplified language of television. Television has given us a new image-based epistemology. It now subtly defines what is true. It determines what constitutes knowledge. It tells us what is real and unreal.

At the same time, television is meant to be incoherent. It bombards us with constantly changing images, colors and sounds. It cleverly sculpts emotion and swings us within seconds from tragedy to excitement to farce to triviality. Television, as Postman wrote, "is transforming our culture into one vast arena for show business." [25] The danger we face is not an Orwellian 1984-style dictatorship, but Aldous Huxley's Brave New World, where we waste our lives in the vain and impossible pursuit of a self-centered, universal happiness.

"What Orwell feared were those who would ban books," Postman wrote:

What Huxley feared was that there would be no reason to ban a book, for there would be no one who wanted to read one. Orwell feared those who would deprive us of information. Huxley feared those who would give us so much that we would be reduced to passivity and egoism. Orwell feared that the truth would be concealed from us. Huxley feared the truth would be drowned in a sea of irrelevance. Orwell feared we would become a captive culture. Huxley feared we would become a trivial culture, preoccupied with some equivalent of the feelies, the orgy porgy, and the centrifugal bumblepuppy. As Huxley remarked in *Brave New World Revisited*, the civil libertarians and rationalists who are ever on the alert to oppose tyranny 'failed to take into account man's almost infinite appetite for distractions.' In *1984*, Huxley added, people are controlled by inflicting pain. In *Brave New World*, they are controlled by inflicting pleasure. In short, Orwell feared that what we hate will ruin us. Huxley feared that what we love will ruin us.[26]

The tens of millions of impoverished Americans in the working class, whose lives and concerns rarely make it on television, have become largely invisible. Shows such as *Cashmere Mafia*, *Big Shots* or *Cane* openly celebrate excess and wealth. Television tempts viewers with the opulent life enjoyed by the American oligarchy, one percent of whom control more wealth than the bottom 90 percent combined. Characters on television live in sprawling and artfully decorated lofts and multimillion-dollar homes. They flit from high-priced luncheons to lavish galas, where they can parade their sculpted bodies in extravagant designer suits and gowns. This is the life we are supposed to admire and emulate. This is the life, we are told, we can all have.

Our national obsession with wealth, celebrity and power has become a soul-crushing disease. Alain de Botton in his book *Status Anxiety* argues that in the Middle Ages people were manipulated and informed by stained glass images and graphic paintings of religious suffering and redemption. We, too, are hostage to images. We are inundated with pictures of excess wealth and consumption. The pious in the Middle Ages genuflected before the awful authority and majesty of the church. They feared the wrath of God. We genuflect before celebrity, prizes, money and status, held out to us like bait. Profligate consumption is not only desirable, but also the only life that offers worth and meaning. These images, however, implicitly mock the lives of nearly all Americans. They foster impossible aspirations, ones that nearly all of us will never achieve. The mass of citizens who do not become wealthy and powerful, who buy Tom Ford's products but never become him, harbor feelings of failure and worthlessness.

The incessant chasing after status and wealth has plunged much of the country into unmanageable debt. Families live in oversized houses with palladium windows, financed with mortgages they cannot repay. They seek identity through their Nike shoes or Coach handbags. They occupy their leisure time in malls buying things they do not need. They spend their weekdays in little cubicles, if they have stable jobs, under the heel of corporations who have disempowered the American worker, taken control of the state, and can lay them off on a whim. It is a desperate scramble. No one wants to be left behind. The epistemology of television has left us ignorant, without the vocabulary to express this awful transformation.

"The evil that is in the world always comes of ignorance, and good intentions may do as much harm as malevolence, if they lack understanding," wrote Albert Camus in *The Plague*. "On the whole, men are more good than bad; that, however, isn't the real point. But they are more or less ignorant, and it is this that we call vice or virtue; the most incorrigible vice being that of an ignorance that fancies it knows everything and therefore claims for itself the right to kill." [27]

The contemporary atheists, while many are noted scientists, are deluded products of this image-based and culturally illiterate world. They speak about religion, human progress and meaning in the impoverished language of television slogans. They play to our fears, especially of what we do not understand. Their words are sensational, fragmented and devoid of content. They appeal to our subliminal and irrational desires. They select a few facts and use them to dismiss historical, political and cultural realities. They tell us what we want to believe about ourselves. They assure us that we are good. They proclaim the violence employed in our name a virtue. They champion our ignorance as knowledge. They assure us that there is no reason to investigate other ways of being. Our way of life is the best. They indulge us in our delusional dream of human perfectibility. They tell us we will be saved by science and rationality. They tell us that humanity is moving inexorably forward. None of this is true. It defies human nature and human history. But it is what we want to believe.

"Nothing worth doing is completed in our lifetime, therefore, we are saved by hope," Reinhold Niebuhr wrote. "Nothing true or beautiful or good makes complete sense in any immediate context of history; Therefore, we are saved by faith. Nothing we do, however virtuous, can be accomplished alone. Therefore, we are saved by love. No virtuous act is quite as virtuous from the standpoint of our friend or foe as from our own; Therefore, we are saved by the final form of love, which is forgiveness."[28]

Religious thought is a guide to morality. It points humans toward inquiry. It seeks to unfetter the mind from prejudices that blunt reflection and self-criticism. We are all flawed. Human ambitions and pursuits are vanity. The ancient Greeks held in high esteem the command they believed came from Apollo: "Know thyself." To know ourselves is to accept our limitations and imperfections. It is to reject absolutism. Ideas are not coded information transmitted like DNA. They are fragile and need to be nurtured and protected. We are bound to this Earth by our common urges and instincts, our capacity to be moral and immoral. It is when we face the intractable nature of our being that we begin to build a viable system of ethics. Utopian dreamers, lifting up impossible ideals, plunge us into depravity and violence. It is those who are broken, those who see the shifting sands of our inner lives and the fictive narratives we hide behind, who can save us. They speak to our common humanity. They appeal to our humility. They talk not of power but of the transcendent. They talk of reverence. And in their words we see the limits of reason and the possibilities of religion.

NOTES

Epigraph

1. Ludwig Feuerbach, *The Essence of Christianity*, trans. George Eliot (New York: Harper and Row, [1855], 1957), reprinted in *Theories of Religion: A Reader*, eds. Seth D. Kunin and Jonathan Miles-Watson (New Brunswick, NJ: Rutgers University Press, 2006), 43.

Chapter One: The God Debate

1. Johann Wolfgang von Goethe, *Faust*, 2.1, "Dark Gallery." Quoted in Thornton Wilder, *The Ides of March* (New York: HarperCollins, 1987), ix.
2. Marcel Proust, *In Search of Lost Time* (New York: Modern Library, 1992), 2:252.
3. United Nations. Department of Economic and Social Affairs. Population Division. "World Population Prospects: Population Database." 10 November 2007. http://esa.un.org/unpp/p2k0data.asp
4. Joseph Conrad, *Victory* (Garden City, NY: Doubleday, 1956), 78.
5. Sam Harris, *The End of Faith: Religion, Terror, and the Future of Reason* (New York: W. W. Norton, 2004), 52–53.
6. Joyce Peseroff, ed., *Simply Lasting: Writers on Jane Kenyon* (Saint Paul, MN: Graywolf Press, 2005), 81.
7. Karen Armstrong, *A History of God* (New York: Ballantine, 1993), xx.
8. Ibid.
9. Karen Armstrong. Interview by Steve Paulson. "Going Beyond God." *Salon*, 30 May 2005. http://www.salon.com/books/int/2006/5/30/armstrong/index_np.html

10. William Shakespeare, *Julius Caesar*, 1.2. 146–47. Ed. Lawrence Mason, in Wilbur L. Cross and Tucker Brooke, eds., *The Yale Shakespeare* (New York: Barnes and Noble, 1993), 947.

11. Richard Dawkins, *The God Delusion* (New York: Houghton Mifflin, 2006), 361.

12. Christopher Hitchens, *God Is Not Great: How Religion Poisons Everything* (New York: Twelve, 2007), 283.

13. Ibid., 282.

14. Dawkins, *The God Delusion*, 270–271.

15. John Gray, *Heresies: Against Progress and Other Illusions* (London: Granta, 2004). 106–107.

16. Reinhold Niebuhr, *Beyond Tragedy* (New York: Charles Scribner's Sons, 1965), 237.

17. Hitchens, *God Is Not Great*, 176.

18. Ibid., 7.

19. Wilhelm Schmidt, *The Origin and Growth of Religion* (New York: Dial, 1931), 6.

20. Harris, *The End of Faith*, 129.

21. Reinhold Niebuhr, *The Irony of American History* (New York: Charles Scribner's Sons, 1952), 21–22.

22. Reinhold Niebuhr, *The Essential Reinhold Niebuhr: Selected Essays and Addresses*, ed. Robert McAfee Brown (New Haven: Yale University Press, 1986), xxi.

23. Karl Popper, *The Open Society and Its Enemies* (Princeton: Princeton University Press, 1971), 1:121.

24. Ibid., 1:122–123.

25. Dawkins, *The God Delusion*, 265.

26. Ibid., 271.

Chapter Two: Science and Religion

1. Albert Einstein, in *Science, Philosophy and Religion, A Symposium* (New York: Conference on Science, Philosophy and Religion in Their Relation to the Democratic Way of Life, 1941), 211. Quoted in http://www.sacred-texts.com/aor/einstein/einsci.htm

2. Leonard Huxley, *Life and Letters of Thomas Henry Huxley* (New York: D. Appleton, 1901), 199.

3. Charles Darwin, *The Descent of Man, and Selection in Relation to Sex.* 2d ed. (1874; reprint 2004, Whitefish MT: Kessinger), 119.

4. Ibid., 117.

5. Curtis Cate, *Friedrich Nietzsche* (Woodstock and New York: Overlook, 2005), 355.

6. Ibid., 355–356.

7. Edward O. Wilson, *On Human Nature* (Cambridge, MA: Harvard University Press, 1978), 188.

8. Edward O. Wilson, *Consilience* (New York: Knopf, 1998), 270. Quoted in John Gray, *Straw Dogs: Thoughts on Humans and Other Animals* (London: Granta, 1995), 5.

9. Richard Dawkins, *The Selfish Gene* (Oxford: Oxford University Press, 1989), 201.

10. Darwin, *Descent of Man*, 93.

11. Leon Trotsky, "Literature and Revolution," in *The Leon Trotsky Internet Archive.* http://www.marxists.org/archive/trotsky/1924/lit_revo/ch08.htm

12. Letter to Cunninghame Graham, 8 February 1899, in Jean Aubrey, *Joseph Conrad Life and Letters* (London: William Heinemann, 1927), 1:269.

13. Ibid.

14. Bertrand Russell, *Portraits from Memory* (London: Allen and Unwin, 1956), 90. Cited in Gray, *Heresies*, 102.

15. Bertrand Russell, *Portraits from Memory* (London: Allen and Unwin, 1956), 87.

16. Kenneth R. Miller, *Finding Darwin's God: A Scientist's Search for Common Ground Between God and Evolution* (New York: Harper, 1999), 200.

17. Quoted in Nick Herbert, *Quantum Reality* (New York: Anchor, 1997), 55.

Chapter Three: The New Fundamentalism

1. Cited in Richard Ellman, *James Joyce* (Oxford: Oxford University Press, 1983), 89.
2. Hitchens, *God Is Not Great*, 71.
3. See Eugene McCarrahar, "This Book Is Not Good," *Commonweal* 134:12 (June 15, 2007).
4. Hitchens, *God Is Not Great*, 7.
5. For a full video of the Hedges–Harris debate: "A/V Booth: Religion, Politics, and the End of the World." *Truthdig.* Posted 17 June 2007. http://www.truthdig.com/avbooth/item/20070617_religion_politics_and_the_end_of_the_world
6. Baruch Spinoza, "Of the Foundations of a State," in *The Chief Works of Benedictus de Spinoza*, ed. Robert Harvey Monro Elwes (London: G. Bell, 1891). 201. Quoted in John Gray, review of Peter Watson, *Ideas: A History from Fire to Freud*, in *The New Statesman*, 30 May 2005. http://www.newstatesman.com/200505300041
7. Omer Bartov, *Murder in Our Midst: The Holocaust, Industrial Killing, and Representation* (New York: Oxford University Press, 1996), 67.
8. James Luther Adams, *The Essential James Luther Adams: Selected Essays and Addresses*, ed. George Kimmich Beach (Boston: Skinner House, 1998), 71.
9. John Ralston Saul, *The Unconscious Civilization* (New York: Free Press, 1995), 2.
10. Ibid., 3.
11. Albert Camus, *The Rebel* (New York, Vintage, 1991), 75.
12. Edward Stillman and William Pfaff, *The Politics of Hysteria: The Sources of Twentieth-Century Conflict* (New York: Harper and Row, 1964), 30.
13. Friedrich Nietzsche, *Thus Spoke Zarathustra* (London: Penguin, 1969), 46.
14. Ibid., 47.
15. Ibid.
16. Friedrich Nietzsche, *Genealogy of Morals*, trans. Horace B. Samuel (New York: Modern Library, 1927), 147–148.
17. Charles Bernheimer, *Flaubert and Kafka: Studies in Psychopoetic Structure* (New Haven: Yale University Press, 1982), 232.

Chapter Four: Self-Delusion

1. Reinhold Niebuhr, *The Irony of American History*, 174.
2. Hitchens, *God Is Not Great*, 180.
3. Ibid., 175.
4. Ibid.
5. Ibid., 176.
6. I taped Parsley saying these words in a talk he gave in Washington, D.C., in March 2006.
7. Samuel Beckett, *Molloy* (New York: Random House, 1997), 37.
8. Ibid., 17.
9. Ibid., 97.
10. Ibid., 57.
11. Ibid., 31–32.
12. Blaise Pascal, *Pensées* (New York: Modern Library, 1941), 23.
13. Cited by Gabriel Josipovici in the introduction of Samuel Beckett, *Malloy, Malone Dies and The Unnamable* (New York: Random House, 1997), xii–xiii.
14. Sam Harris, *Letter to a Christian Nation* (New York: Knopf, 2006), 85.
15. Daniel Dennett, *Darwin's Dangerous Idea* (New York: Simon & Schuster, 1995), 21.
16. Ibid., 515.
17. Varlam Shalamov, *Kolyma Tales* (New York: Penguin, 1994), 22.
18. Ibid., 32.
19. Wolfgang Sofsky, *The Order of Terror: The Concentration Camp*, trans. William Templer (Princeton: Princeton University Press, 1997), 167–168.
20. Primo Levi, *The Drowned and the Saved* (New York: Vintage, 1989), 69.
21. William Pfaff, *The Bullet's Song: Romantic Violence and Utopia* (New York: Simon & Schuster, 2004), 306.
22. Jocelyn Baines, *Joseph Conrad: A Critical Biography* (New York: Penguin, 1986), 529–530.

Chapter Five: The Myth of Moral Progress

1. Reinhold Niebuhr, *The Nature and Destiny of Man* (Louisville: Westminster John Knox, 1996), 1:24.
2. Sigmund Freud, *Civilization and Its Discontents* (New York: W.W. Norton, 1989), 68–69.
3. Tzvetan Todorov, *Hope and Memory: Lessons from the Twentieth Century* (Princeton: Princeton University Press, 2000), 27.
4. Niebuhr, *The Essential Reinhold Niebuhr*, 105.
5. Ibid., 104–105.
6. Freud, *Civilization and Its Discontents*, 69.
7. Harris, *The End of Faith*, 151.
8. Niebuhr, *Beyond Tragedy*, 39.
9. John Gray, *Black Mass: Apocalyptic Religion and the Death of Utopia* (London: Penguin, 2007), 193.

Chapter Six: Humiliation and Revenge

1. Fyodor Dostoevsky, "The Dream of a Ridiculous Man," in *A Gentle Creature and Other Stories*, trans. Alan Myers (Oxford: Oxford University Press World's Classics, 1995), 125.
2. Harris, *The End of Faith*, 110.
3. Robert Jay Lifton, "American Apocalypse," *The Nation*, December 2003. http://www.thenation.com/doc/20031222/lifton
4. Ibid.
5. Ibid.
6. Robert Pape. Interview by Scott McConnell. "The Logic of Suicide Terrorism," *The American Conservative* 18 July 2005. http://www.amconmag.com/2005_07_18/article.html
7. Lifton, "American Apocalypse."
8. Dawkins, *The God Delusion*, 308.
9. Fyodor Dostoevsky, *Crime and Punishment* (New York: Knopf, 1993), 547.
10. Ibid.
11. Ibid.
12. Joseph Conrad, *Heart of Darkness* (New York: Penguin, 1989), 55.

13. Ibid., 115.
14. Ibid., 47
15. Ibid., 86–87.
16. Tadatoshi Akiba, mayor of Hiroshima. Peace Declaration. August 6, 2007. http://www.pcf.city.hiroshima.jp/declaration/English/index .html
17. Joseph Conrad, "An Outpost of Progress," in *The Portable Conrad*, ed. Morton Dauwen Zaubel (New York: Viking, 1947), 462.
18. Ibid., 489.
19. Harris, *The End of Faith*, 29.
20. Ibid., 194
21. Ibid., 151–152.
22. Ibid., 193.

Chapter 7: The Illusive Self

1. William Shakespeare, *Measure for Measure*, 1.2.144–148, ed. Davis Harding, in *The Yale Shakespeare*, 412–413.
2. Gray, *Straw Dogs*, 66.
3. Arthur Schopenhauer, *The World as Will and Representation*, trans. E. F. J. Payne (New York: Dover, 1969), 1: 238–239. Cited in Gray, *Straw Dogs*, 68.
4. Aristotle, *Poetics*, trans. James Hutton (New York: W. W. Norton, 1982), 54.
5. Willa Cather, *The Song of the Lark* (New York: Vintage, 1999), 278–279.
6. Tzvetan Todorov, *The Conquest of America* (New York: Harper and Row, 1984), 69.
7. Gray, *Straw Dogs*, 62.
8. Uta Hagen, *Respect for Acting* (New York: Macmillan, 1973), 47–48.
9. Uta Hagen, *A Challenge for the Actor* (New York: Scribner, 1991), 88.
10. Marcel Proust, *In Search of Lost Time* (New York: Modern Library, 1992), 1:59–60.
11. Marcel Proust, *In Search of Lost Time* (New York: Modern Library, 1993), 4:211–212.

12. Marcel Proust, *In Search of Lost Time* (New York: Modern Library, 1992), 1:60.
13. Ibid.
14. Ibid., 1:61.
15. Ibid., 1:63.
16. Marcel Proust, *In Search of Lost Time* (New York: Modern Library, 1993), 5:804.
17. Ibid.
18. Ibid., 5:804–805.
19. Ibid., 5:805.
20. Northrop Frye, *The Great Code: The Bible and Literature* (New York: Harcourt, 1982), 123–124.
21. Paul Tillich, *The Courage to Be* (New Haven: Yale University Press, 1952), 190.
22. Joost A.M. Merloo, *The Rape of the Mind: The Psychology of Thought Control, Menticide, and Brainwashing* (New York: World Publishing, 1955), 202.
23. Neil Postman, *Amusing Ourselves to Death: Public Discourse in the Age of Show Business* (New York: Penguin, 1985), 3–4.
24. Marcel Proust, *In Search of Lost Time* (New York: Modern Library, 1992) 2:213.
25. Postman, *Amusing Ourselves to Death*, 80.
26. Ibid., viii.
27. Albert Camus, *The Plague* (New York: Modern Library, 1948), 120–121.
28. Niebuhr, *The Irony of American History*, 63.

BIBLIOGRAPHY

Adams, James Luther. *The Essential James Luther Adams: Selected Essays and Addresses.* Edited by George Kimmich Beach. Boston: Skinner House, 1998.

———. *An Examined Faith: Social Context and Religious Commitment.* Edited by George Kimmich Beach. Boston: Beacon, 1991.

———. *On Being Human Religiously.* Boston: Beacon, 1976.

———. *Paul Tillich's Philosophy of Culture, Science, and Religion.* New York: Harper and Row, 1965.

Arendt, Hannah. *The Origins of Totalitarianism.* San Diego: Harcourt, 1976.

Aristotle. *Poetics.* Translated by James Hutton. New York: W. W. Norton, 1982.

Armstrong, Karen. *The Battle for God: A History of Fundamentalism.* New York: Random House, 2000.

———. *The Great Transformation: The Beginning of Our Religious Traditions.* New York: Anchor, 2006.

———. *A History of God.* New York: Ballantine, 1993

Aubry, Jean. *Joseph Conrad Life and Letters.* vol. 1. London: Heinemann, 1927.

Beckett, Samuel. *Molloy, Malone Dies, The Unnamable.* New York: Everyman's Library, 1997.

———. *Samuel Beckett: The Grove Centenary Edition. Volume 3: Dramatic Works.* New York: Grove, 2006.

Baines, Jocelyn. *Joseph Conrad: A Critical Biography.* New York: Penguin, 1986.

Bartov, Omer. *Mirrors of Destruction: War, Genocide, and Modern Identity.* Oxford: Oxford University Press, 2000.

———. *Murder in Our Midst: The Holocaust, Industrial Killing, and Representation.* New York: Oxford University Press, 1996.

Bernheimer, Charles. *Flaubert and Kafka: Studies in Psychopoetic Structure*. New Haven: Yale University Press, 1982.

Bonhoeffer, Dietrich. *The Cost of Discipleship*. New York: Touchstone, 1995.

Camus, Albert. *The Plague*. New York: Modern Library, 1948.

———. *The Rebel*. New York: Vintage, 1991.

Canetti, Elias. *Crowds and Power*. New York: Farrar, Straus and Giroux, 1984.

Carter, Stephen L. *The Culture of Disbelief: How American Law and Politics Trivialize Religious Devotion*. New York: Anchor, 1994.

Cate, Curtis. *Friedrich Nietzsche*. Woodstock: Overlook, 2002.

Cather, Willa. *The Song of the Lark*. New York, Vintage, 1999.

Cohn, Norman. *The Pursuit of the Millennium*. New York: Oxford University Press, 1970.

Conrad, Joseph. *Heart of Darkness*. London: Penguin, 1989.

———. *Lord Jim*. London: Everyman, 1992.

———. *The Portable Conrad*. Edited by Morton Dauwen Zabel. New York: Viking, 1947.

———. *Victory*. New York: Doubleday, 1957.

Darwin, Charles. *The Descent of Man, and Selection in Relation to Sex*. 2d Edition. 1874. Reprinted Whitefish MT: Kessinger, 2004.

Dawkins, Richard. *The God Delusion*. Boston: Houghton Mifflin, 2006.

———. *The Selfish Gene*. Oxford: Oxford University Press, 1989.

Dennett, Daniel C. *Breaking the Spell: Religion as a Natural Phenomenon*. New York: Viking, 2006.

Dostoevsky, Fyodor. *Crime and Punishment*. New York: Knopf, 1993.

———. *Demons*. New York: Knopf, 2000.

———. "The Dream of a Ridiculous Man," in *A Gentle Creature and Other Stories*. Translated by Alan Myers. Oxford: Oxford University Press, 1995.

Ellmann, Richard. *James Joyce*. Oxford: Oxford University Press, 1983.

Feuerbach, Ludwig. *The Essence of Christianity*. Translated by George Eliot. 1855. Reprinted in *Theories of Religion: A Reader*. Edited by Seth D. Kunin with Jonathan Miles-Watson. New Brunswick, NJ: Rutgers University Press, 2006

Foucault, Michel. *The Archaeology of Knowledge and the Discourse on Language*. New York: Pantheon, 1972.

Freud, Sigmund. *Civilization and Its Discontents.* New York: W. W. Norton, 1989.

Frye, Northrop. *The Great Code: The Bible and Literature.* San Diego: Harcourt, 1982.

Goethe, Johann Wolfgang von. *Faust.* New York: W. W. Norton, 2001.

Gray, John. *Black Mass: Apocalyptic Religion and the Death of Utopia.* London: Allen Lane, 2007.

———. *Enlightenment's Wake.* London: Routledge, 1995.

———. *Heresies: Against Progress and Other Illusions.* London: Granta, 2004.

———. *Liberalism.* Minneapolis, University of Minnesota Press, 1995.

———. *Straw Dogs: Thoughts on Humans and Other Animals.* London: Granta, 2002.

Hagen, Uta. *Respect for Acting.* New York: Macmillan, 1973.

Harris, Sam. *The End of Faith: Religion, Terror, and the Future of Reason.* New York: W. W. Norton, 2004.

———. *Letter to a Christian Nation.* New York: Knopf, 2006.

Hedges, Chris. *American Fascists: The Christian Right and the War on America.* New York: Free Press, 2006.

Herbert, Nick. *Quantum Reality.* New York: Anchor, 1997.

Heschel, Abraham J. *Between God and Man: An Interpretation of Judaism.* New York: Free Press, 1997.

Hitchens, Christopher. *God Is Not Great: How Religion Poisons Everything.* New York: Twelve, 2007.

Hughes, Richard T. *Myths America Lives By.* Chicago: University of Illinois Press, 2003.

Huxley, Leonard. *Life and Letters of Thomas Henry Huxley.* vol. 1. New York: D. Appleton, 1901.

Joyce, James. *Ulysses.* New York: Modern Library, 1992.

Kierkegaard, Søren. *Either/Or.* vol. 1. Princeton: Princeton University Press, 1971.

———. *Either/Or.* vol. 2. Princeton: Princeton University Press, 1974.

Levi, Primo. *The Drowned and the Saved.* New York: Vintage, 1989.

Meerloo, Joost A. M. *The Rape of the Mind: The Psychology of Thought Control, Menticide, and Brainwashing.* Cleveland: World, 1956.

Miles, Jack. *God: A Biography.* New York: Vintage, 1996.

Miller, Kenneth R. *Finding Darwin's God: A Scientist's Search for Common Ground Between God and Evolution*. New York: Harper Perennial, 1999.

Niebuhr, Reinhold. *Beyond Tragedy*. New York: Charles Scribner's Sons, 1965.

———. *The Children of Light and the Children of Darkness: A Vindication of Democracy and a Critique of Its Traditional Defense*. New York: Charles Scribner's Sons, 1950.

———. *The Essential Reinhold Niebuhr: Selected Essays and Addresses*. Edited by Robert McAfee Brown. New Haven: Yale University Press, 1986.

———. *Faith and History*. New York: Charles Scribner's Sons, 1949.

———. *An Interpretation of Christian Ethics*. San Francisco: HarperSanFrancisco, 1963.

———. *The Irony of American History*. New York: Charles Scribner's Sons, 1952

———. *Justice and Mercy*. Edited by Ursula M. Niebuhr. Louisville, KY: Westminster John Knox, 1974.

———. *Love and Justice: Selections from the Shorter Writings of Reinhold Niebuhr*. Edited by D. B. Robertson. Louisville, KY: Westminster John Knox, 1957.

———. *Moral Man and Immoral Society: A Study in Ethics and Politics*. Louisville, KY: Westminster John Knox, 2001.

———. *The Nature and Destiny of Man: A Christian Interpretation*. vol. 1. Louisville, KY: Westminster John Knox, 1996.

———. *The Nature and Destiny of Man: A Christian Interpretation*. vol. 2. Louisville, KY: Westminster John Knox, 1964.

Niebuhr, H. Richard. *Christ and Culture*. San Francisco: HarperSanFrancisco, 2001.

Nietzsche, Friedrich. *The Genealogy of Morals*. Edited by Horace B. Samuel. New York: Modern Library, 1927.

Nietzsche, Friedrich. *Thus Spoke Zarathustra*. London: Penguin, 1969.

Pascal, Blaise. *Pensées*. New York: Modern Library, 1941.

Pfaff, William. *Barbarian Sentiments: America in the New Century*. New York: Hill and Wang, 2000.

———. *The Bullet's Song: Romantic Violence and Utopia*. New York: Simon & Schuster, 2004.

———. *The Wrath of Nations: Civilization and the Furies of Nationalism*. New York: Touchstone, 1993.

Pfaff, William, and Edmund Stillman. *The Politics of Hysteria: The Sources of Twentieth-Century Conflict.* New York: Harper and Row, 1964.

Popper, Karl R. *The Open Society and Its Enemies.* vol. 1. Princeton: Princeton University Press, 1966.

———. *The Open Society and Its Enemies.* vol. 2. Princeton: Princeton University Press, 1966.

Peseroff, Joyce, ed. *Simply Lasting: Writers on Jane Kenyon.* Saint Paul, MN: Graywolf, 2005.

Postman, Neil. *Amusing Ourselves to Death: Public Discourse in the Age of Show Business.* New York: Penguin, 1985.

Proust, Marcel. *In Search of Lost Time.* vol. 1. Translated by C.K. Scott Moncrieff and Terence Kilmartin. New York: Modern Library, 1992.

———. *In Search of Lost Time.* vol. 2. Translated by C. K. Scott Moncrieff and Terence Kilmartin. New York: Modern Library, 1992.

———. *In Search of Lost Time.* vol. 3. Translated by C. K. Scott Moncrieff and Terence Kilmartin. New York: Modern Library, 1993.

———. *In Search of Lost Time.* vol. 4. Translated by C. K. Scott Moncrieff and Terence Kilmartin. New York: Modern Library, 1993.

———. *In Search of Lost Time.* vol. 5. Translated by C. K. Scott Moncrieff and Terence Kilmartin. New York: Modern Library, 1993.

———. *In Search of Lost Time.* Vol. 6. Translated by C. K. Scott Moncrieff and Terence Kilmartin. New York: Modern Library, 1993.

Russell, Bertrand. *Portraits from Memory and Other Essays.* London: Allen and Unwin, 1956.

———. *Why I Am Not a Christian.* New York: Touchstone, 1957.

Saul, John Ralston. *The Unconscious Civilization.* New York: Free Press, 1997.

Schmidt, Wilhelm. *The Origin and Growth of Religion.* 1931. Reprinted 1957 in *Theories of Religion: A Reader.* Edited by Seth D. Kunin with Jonathan Miles-Watson. New Brunswick, NJ: Rutgers University Press, 2006

Science, Philosophy and Religion: A Symposium. New York: Conference on Science, Philosophy and Religion in Their Relation to the Democratic Way of Life, Inc. 1941.

Shakespeare, William. *The Riverside Shakespeare.* 2d ed. Edited by G. Blakemore Evans and J. J. M. Tobin. Boston: Houghton Mifflin, 1997.

Shalamov, Varlam. *Kolyma Tales*. New York: Penguin, 1994.

Sofsky, Wolfgang. *The Order of Terror: The Concentration Camp*. Translated by William Templer. Princeton: Princeton University Press, 1997.

Tillich, Paul. *The Courage to Be*. New Haven: Yale Nota Bene, 2000.

Todorov, Tzvetan. *The Conquest of America*. New York: Harper and Row, 1984.

———. *Facing the Extreme: Moral Life in the Concentration Camps*. New York: Henry Holt, 1996.

———. *Hope and Memory: Lessons from the Twentieth Century*. Princeton: Princeton University Press, 2003.

Wilder, Thornton. *The Ides of March*. New York: HarperCollins, 1987.

Wilson, David Sloan. *Darwin's Cathedral: Evolution, Religion, and the Nature of Society*. Chicago: University of Chicago Press, 2002.

Wilson, Edward O. *Consilience: The Unity of Knowledge*. New York: Knopf, 1998.

———. *On Human Nature*. Cambridge: Harvard University Press, 1978.

Woodruff, Paul. *Reverence: Renewing a Forgotten Virtue*. Oxford: Oxford University Press, 2001.

ACKNOWLEDGMENTS

This book was possible because of generous assistance from The Nation Institute and the Lannan Foundation. The support permitted me to research and write this work. I owe much to Hamilton Fish, Taya Grobow, Esther Kaplan and Jonathan Schell, as well as Peggy Suttle and Katrina vanden Heuvel at *The Nation* magazine. I would also like to thank Patrick Lannan, who is the patron saint of writers, and Jo Chapman.

Eunice Wong worked on all phases of this book. She carefully edited every page, most more than once, and helped me articulate the larger concepts and ideas. She reorganized material, cut with ruthless efficiency and left the imprint of her brilliance on the manuscript. It was collaboration, as is our marriage. I am fortunate beyond words. The Reverend Coleman Brown, as he has for every book I have written, offered his wisdom and guidance from the start to the finish of the book. Chapters made their way in express packages to Hamilton, New York, and came back with Coleman's penetrating insights and frank critique in the margins. It is a better and more nuanced book because of him. I am once again deeply in his debt. John Timpane, without question the finest editor I have ever worked with, did the final edit of the book. John combines the rare talents of being able to line-edit in detail and then step back and take apart the central argument with stunning and penetrating insight. He has a towering intellect, but more importantly is a lover of books and a great friend. I write into my book contracts that John, and John alone, will be the last person to edit my work. I would not want to do this without him.

The genesis of the book came when Robert Scheer and Zuade Kaufmann asked me to debate Sam Harris at UCLA. Robert, an icon of journalistic integrity, and Zuade run Truthdig, a great Web site that upholds the best traditions of American journalism and commentary. They allow me to write a biweekly column for them. I am thankful for their support and friendship. I owe thanks to Bernard Rapoport, a great Texan, Jean Stein, Ralph Nader, Larry Joseph, Steve Kinzer, Laila al–Arian, Cristina Nehring, Peter Scheer, Ann and Walter Pincus, Lauren B. Davis, June Ballinger, Michael Goldstein, Rick McArthur, Anne Marie Macari, Robert J. Lifton, Richard Fenn, Irene Brown, Sam and Liz Hynes, Joe Sacco, Mae Sakharov, Kasia Anderson, Steve Burkard, Charlie and Catherine Williams, the wonderful Reverend Mel White (who married us on a beach on Fire Island), the Reverend Davidson Loehr, the Reverend Ed Bacon, Bishop Krister Stendhal, the Reverend Joe Hough, the Reverend Michael Granzen, Gail and Stan Scott, who let us return to Summit Study, and the Reverend Terry Burke. Gerald Stern, one of the nation's finest poets, worked with me on the first chapters of the book to give them clarity. I am thankful for his friendship and his prodigious insight and brilliance as a poet and a thinker.

My editors at the Free Press, especially Dominick Anfuso and Leah Miller, patiently helped edit and organize the book. I would also like to thank Nicole Kalian, who tirelessly works to keep my work before the public. Lisa Bankoff of International Creative Management, for the fifth time, handled this book with her usual charm, intelligence and efficiency.

And finally, I again have to thank Eunice, along with Thomas, Noëlle, Konrad, and our shaggy dog Holly. They are my family. They matter most. This is just a book. They are my life.

INDEX

ABOUT THE AUTHOR

CHRIS HEDGES, who graduated from seminary at Harvard Divinity School, was a foreign correspondent for nearly two decades for *The New York Times* and other publications. He was part of the team of reporters at *The New York Times* that won the 2002 Pulitzer Prize for its coverage of global terrorism. Hedges has taught at Princeton University and Columbia University and is the author of *New York Times* bestseller *American Fascists, War Is a Force That Gives Us Meaning* and *Losing Moses on the Freeway: The 10 Commandments in America.* He lives in Princeton, New Jersey.